Flight & Bliss

Flight & Bliss

Two plays by
Mikhail Bulgakov

Translated from the Russian by Mirra Ginsburg

A NEW DIRECTIONS BOOK

This translation . Flight was first published by Grove Press in 1969; it
was originally published by Iskusstvo, Moscow, 1962; Bliss first appeared
in Zvezda Vostoka, Uzbekistan, 1966.

Manufactured in the United States of America
First published in cloth and as New Directions Paperbook 593 in 1985
Published simultaneously in Canada by Penguin Books Canada Limited

Library of Congress Cataloging in Publication Data

Bulgakov, Mikhail Afanaśevich, 1891–1940.
  Flight ; & Bliss.
  (A New Directions Book)
  Translation of: Beg and Blazhenstvo.
  1. Bulgakov, Mikhail Afanaśevich, 1891–1940—
Translations, English. I. Bulgakov, Mikhail Afanaśevich, 1891–1940.
Blazhenstvo. English. 1985. II. Ginsburg, Mirra. III. Title: Flight. IV.
Title: Bliss.
PG3476.B78B43 1985   891.72′42   84–29445

New Directions Books are published for James Laughlin
by New Directions Publishing Corporation
80 Eighth Avenue, New York 10011
SECOND PRINTING

TABLE OF CONTENTS

INTRODUCTION

Mikhail Bulgakov (1891–1940) is known in this country chiefly as a brilliant novelist, the author of *The Master and Margarita*,[1] the satires, *Heart of a Dog*[2] and *The Fatal Eggs*,[3] and other prose works.

Ironically, in the Soviet Union Bulgakov was known for many years chiefly as a playwright. This anomalous situation was the result, not of literary preferences, but of the political exigencies of the time. Bulgakov himself, a passionately dedicated artist, felt that he needed both the fictional and the dramatic forms, "just as a pianist needs both his right and left hand."

The son of a professor at the Kiev Theological Academy and a physician by training, Bulgakov gave up medicine after a short period of practice to devote himself entirely to writing. He came to Moscow in 1921 and plunged into the teeming literary life of the time. During his first years in the hungry and ravaged capital, he earned his liv-

[1] Mikhail Bulgakov, *The Master and Margarita*, translated by Mirra Ginsburg. New York: Grove Press, 1967.

[2] Mikhail Bulgakov, *Heart of a Dog*, translated by Mirra Ginsburg. New York: Grove Press, 1968.

[3] *The Fatal Eggs and Other Soviet Satire*, translated and edited by Mirra Ginsburg. New York: Macmillan Publishing Co., 1965.

ing by journalistic work, while doing his more serious writing at night. In 1925 he published a collection of satirical tales, *The Diaboliad*, and began publication of a novel, *The White Guard*, in the journal *Rossiya*. Like many other literary ventures of that time, *Rossiya* soon folded, and only the first two parts of the novel appeared in print (it was not published in Soviet Russia in full until 1966). However, these parts were enough to unleash a storm of criticism and abuse from Communist circles.

In the relatively freer mid-1920's it was still possible for the Moscow Art Theater to disregard the criticism and invite Bulgakov to dramatize the novel. The resulting play, *The Days of the Turbins*, was presented in 1926, with instant and enormous success.

Like the novel, the play came under virulent attack. It dealt with the last days of the Civil War which followed the revolution in Russia. Its characters were Russian intellectuals and White officers. What particularly incensed the Communist and Proletarian critics was Bulgakov's treatment of these characters as sympathetic and doomed human beings rather than as stock images of "the class enemy." In endless attacks, Bulgakov was branded an apologist for the Whites, a petty-bourgeois counter-revolutionary, and an anti-Soviet writer whose works had no place in revolutionary Russia.

By 1929 Bulgakov was totally barred both from publication and the stage. He was strenuously advised from all sides by "well-wishers" to write a "Communist play" and to send a letter to the government, confessing and recanting his sins. Instead, in March of 1930, he wrote a letter of remarkable courage, tracing his literary career, quoting his critics, and agreeing that his works, indeed, had no place in the Soviet Union.

In this letter, he wrote that the Glavrepertkom (the

Chief Repertory Committee or censorship organ) was killing creative thought and destroying Soviet drama. He wrote: "I regard it my duty as a writer to fight censorship, in whatever form and under whatever government it may exist, and to call for freedom of the press. . . . Any writer who tries to prove that he has no need for creative freedom is like a fish publicly declaring that it needs no water." He wrote that he had become a satirist at a time when true satire, which penetrates into forbidden zones, was absolutely unthinkable in the Soviet Union. He also described himself as a mystical writer, and as a man who regarded the Russian intelligentsia as the best stratum of Russian society.

In the final paragraphs of this letter, he said: "To me, impossibility to write is tantamount to being buried alive." He therefore requested the Soviet government, in all humanity, to allow him, a writer who could not be useful in his own homeland, to leave the country.

But, he went on to say, if all that he had written was not sufficiently convincing and he was condemned to silence as a writer in the USSR, he begged the government to assign him to work in his other field, the theater— as a director, or an actor—or, if that was impossible, as an extra, or even a stagehand.

It is said that Stalin himself telephoned Bulgakov from the Kremlin and arranged for his appointment as assistant director at the Moscow Art Theater.

Flight was written during 1926–1928. Initially, it had been accepted for production by the Moscow Art Theater, the only theater in the country that received permission to produce it. Two weeks later, when it was in rehearsal (with some of the greatest actors of the time), the Glavrepertkom definitively banned it, despite the strong opposition of Gorky, Lunacharsky, Stanislavsky, and others. *Flight* was not produced in Russia until 1957 (in the Gorky Theater in Volgograd). In the summer of 1958 it had its Leningrad première in the Pushkin State Academic Theater.

Flight, though an independent play, may, historically speaking, be regarded as a sequel to *The Days of the Turbins*. It takes up where the earlier play left off. Its characters are different, but the milieu is the same. It opens during the last hours of the Civil War and follows the defeated and escaping Whites into exile, to Constantinople and, briefly, to Paris.

An evocation of the aftermath of defeat of the Tsarist forces in Russia, the play moves swiftly, creating a vivid sense of chaos and disintegration—the tragic turning into comic, the respected and respectable into the disreputable and grotesque.

Like Zamyatin, Blok, Mandelshtam, and other significant writers and poets of the period, Bulgakov possessed an extraordinary sense of history. He was keenly aware of the present as a moment in the constant flow of change, never losing sight, if only implicitly, of the past and the possible future. Hence the prophetic and apocalyptic quality of much of his work.

Both in theme and in treatment, *Flight* is as relevant today as it was at the time of writing. It is a tragicomic picture of man violently uprooted and struggling for some sort of survival—each on his own terms—in an alien, indifferent, if not hostile world. Bulgakov comes close to one of the central problems of our time, the problem of the displaced person, repeated in the course of the past half-century in endless variations—geographic, political, cultural, moral, and philosophic.

The immediate roots of the play are in the realities of the period, and some of its characters are based on actual persons. Thus, the commander in chief is modeled after General Wrangel, who commanded the White

Armies in 1919–1920. Archbishop Africanus is based on Bishop Veniamin. Khludov is based on the notorious General Slashchov, commander of the Wrangel forces in the Crimea in 1920, who returned to Russia with a confession of guilt soon after the rout of the White Armies. (By one of the strange freaks of fate in a time of total upheaval, he was pardoned and reinstated in the army—the Red Army—in which he served loyally until his death.)

The nightmare image of Khludov, which dominates the play, is a portrait of a man who disintegrates as his world disintegrates, a man who is both executioner and victim. It foreshadows that dissolution of moral standards and restraints which made possible the mass extermination of human beings witnessed by the world in subsequent decades.

On the other hand, the hyperbolic image of General Charnota, hell-bent for destruction after his world is destroyed—a masterpiece of portraiture, individual, yet superbly generalized—is tragedy in the mask of laughter.

At the end of the play, which is divided into "dreams" rather than scenes, three go home: the crazed general who sought to stem the new by absolute terror and is returning to expiate his guilt, and the man and woman in love, who have also been corrupted and despairing in the process of flight, but who still retain enough integrity to opt for life and order. And there might well have been a sequel to *Flight*. For "home," as they knew it, is also gone. And so the ending, which might at first glance seem happily sentimental and affirmative, is in reality as ironic as the rest of the play and, indeed, as all of Bulgakov's sharp and satirical works.

Bliss, a pessimistic comedy, is on the surface perhaps one of Mikhail Bulgakov's most light-hearted plays. Unlike *The Days of the Turbins*, a realistic play, and *Flight*, in which the real is carried over into the grotesque, *Bliss* is a cunning blend of fantasy and reality. A satirical-romantic romp through history, it mocks the past, the present, and the "ideal" future envisaged by the present as its goal.

The comedy is marked by the same extravagantly comic imagination as Bulgakov's novel *The Master and Margarita*, and his novellas, *The Fatal Eggs* and *Heart of a Dog*. It abounds in masterly touches. A pickpocket, transported to a crimeless and policeless future, weeps tenderly before the effigy of a policeman in the museum. A house manager "revokes" the housing cards of defunct tenants and reproaches an abandoned husband for failure to report the departure of his unfaithful wife. Everything "must be registered" with the appropriate authorities.

The very choice of names in the comedy is often meaningful. Rein—the pure man, the disinterested scientist (read "artist" or "intellectual") is plagued in the present by the stupid, bureaucratic and ubiquitous Bunshas. In the future, he is persecuted by the equally stupid, bureaucratic and formula-ridden Savvichs, who seek to force life into preconceived ideas of "harmony" and are intolerant of every expression of free, uncontrollable life and emotions. The intellectual, carried into the future, is again compelled to say, "I see. I am a prisoner." Later, on his return to the present, he is marched off under guard by the militia, while Bunsha says reassuringly "Don't be afraid—our militia is kind."

Svyatoslav Vladimirovich Bunsha, a former nobleman whose name and patronymic evoke the hallowed memory of ancient Russian princes, is now a petty police informer who insists, for the sake of safety in the proletarian state, that he is really the illegitimate son of his father's coachman. Yury Miloslavsky, a burglar and a pickpocket, bears the name of an ancient boyar family whose proud members fought Tsar Ivan's attempt to subdue the feudal nobles to autocratic rule and were, in a later century, related by marriage to the royal family.

These names inevitably suggest the question "What has become of old Russia?" and comment wryly on the fragility of human claims to aristocracy. And what could be a clearer reference to the state of Russia at the time of writing than the reappearance of Ivan the Terrible in the present?

All this is done with the lightest of hands, with consummate grace, without for a moment violating the logical illogic of the zany goings-on, which are in themselves a withering commentary on the absurdity of 20th century life and ideals—perhaps of man himself?

Bliss was written in 1934, during the last and most painful decade of Bulgakov's life. Allowed by Stalin's whim to work as assistant director and literary consultant at the Moscow Art Theatre, and later at the Bolshoi, Bulgakov, one of Russia's greatest and most original writers of our century, was confined to dramatizing the novels of other men (including Gogol's *Dead Souls* and Cervantes' *Don Quixote*).

A man of extraordinary courage and creative vitality, he continued his own writing despite inability to reach his audience. Like certain other writers of the time, he turned to history, writing *The Last Days*, a play on Pushkin's death, on which he worked in 1934–1935 (produced only in 1943, three years after Bulgakov's death); *Molière, or the Cabal of the Hypocrites* (written between 1930 and 1936), and a moving biography of the French satirist. He also worked on the *Theatrical Novel* and *The Master and Margarita* (not published until 1965 and 1966 respectively). As in *Bliss*, one of his chief concerns in all these works was the relationship of the artist, the intellectual, with his society and its rulers.

In *The Life of Monsieur de Molière*,[4] written in 1932–1933 (published in 1962), Bulgakov deals repeatedly with the problem of the silenced writer. What was Molière's reaction, he asks, to the ban on *Tartuffe* following the presentation of the first acts at Versailles? "As soon as he recovered from the Versailles scandal, the unrepentant playwright sat down to write the fourth and fifth acts." Elsewhere, he compares the author remaking his work under the pressure of censorship to a lizard breaking off its tail. But the censors, he writes, do not know that "changes in a work cannot alter its essential meaning a single iota."

Bliss, sharply satirical under its playful exterior, obviously had no chance in Stalin's Russia. In 1935–1936, Bulgakov wrote another variation on the theme, *Ivan Vasilievich*, eliminating the picture of the future and shifting much of the action to the time of Tsar Ivan the Terrible. This second play was accepted for production by the Theater of Satire. Its premiere was to take place in 1936. That year seemed to mark a relaxation of the ban on Bulgakov's plays. His Molière (accepted for production in 1932) opened in February, 1936. It was met with a burst of angry criticism and was withdrawn from the repertory of the Moscow Art Theater after seven performances. After that, *Ivan Vasilievich*, already in the stage of dress rehearsal, with tickets selling and premiere scheduled, was also banned. Quite evidently, Bulgakov had underestimated the censors: they did not fail to see that changes in the work had not altered its essential meaning.

Bliss was not included in the small collection of Bulgakov's plays which appeared in the Soviet Union in 1962, following his "rehabilitation," or in the slightly expanded

---

[4] Mikhail Bulgakov, *The Life of Monsieur de Moliere*, translated by Mirra Ginsburg. New York: Funk & Wagnalls Inc., 1970.

edition of 1965, which included *Ivan Vasilievich,* a considerably weaker play. It first appeared in print in 1966, in a monthly *Zvezda Vostoka* ("Star of the East," published in Uzbekistan), which, like some other periodicals of outlying areas, has occasionally carried material that no central Soviet publication would print.

Bulgakov died in 1940 leaving a rich legacy of suppressed works. Today, more than four decades after his death, *Bliss,* a brilliant part of this legacy, is still virtually unknown in Soviet Russia, and known to only a small body of scholars in the West.

MIRRA GINSBURG

Flight

A Play in Eight Dreams & Four Acts

Immortality—a quiet, bright shore;
Our road—a striving toward it.
Rest, all of you whose race is run.
                              —Zhukovsky

SETTING

First Dream: southern Russia in October, 1920
Second, Third, and Fourth Dreams: the Crimea in early
    November, 1920
Fifth and Sixth Dreams: Constantinople in the summer of
    1921
Seventh Dream: Paris in the autumn of 1921
Eighth Dream: Constantinople in the autumn of 1921

CHARACTERS

Serafima Vladimirovna Korzukhina, *a young matron, fleeing from Petersburg*

Sergey Pavlovich Golubkov, *son of an idealist professor, fleeing from Petersburg*

Africanus, *Archbishop of Simferopol and Karasubazar, spiritual leader of the White Armies, alias chemist* MAKHROV

Paisy, *a monk*

Aged Father Superior

Bayev, *commander of a regiment in Budenny's cavalry*

Soldier, *in Budenny's cavalry*

Grigory Lukyanovich Charnota, *Zaporozhe Cossack by origin, cavalryman, Major General of White Army*

Barabanchikova, *a pregnant lady existing solely in General Charnota's imagination*

Lyuska, *General Charnota's camp wife*

Krapilin, *General Charnota's orderly, destroyed by his own eloquence*

De Brizar, *commander of a Hussar regiment of the White Army*

Roman Valerianovich Khludov

Golovan, *Cossack Captain, Khludov's adjutant*

Commandant of railway station

Stationmaster

3

Nikolayevna, *wife of stationmaster*
Olka, *their four-year-old daughter*
Paramon Ilyich Korzukhin, *Serafima's husband, Vice-Minister of Trade*
Tikhy, *chief of counter-intelligence*
Skunsky⎫
Gurin ⎬ *counter-intelligence men*
Commander in Chief of the White Armies
A face in the ticket office
Artur Arturovich, *cockroach king*
Figure in a derby, *with shoulder straps of Quartermaster Corps*
Turkish woman, *a loving mother*
Beautiful prostitute
Greek Don Juan
Antoine Grishchenko, *Korzukhin's valet*

Monks, White staff officers, Cossacks in the convoy of the White Commander in Chief, counter-intelligence men, Cossacks in felt cloaks, British, French and Italian sailors, Turkish and Italian police, Turkish and Greek street urchins, Armenian and Greek heads in windows, crowd in Constantinople.

Act One

I dreamed of a monastery . . .

FIRST DREAM

The muffled sound of a monks' choir comes from the underground vaults, singing "Holy Saint Nicholas, pray to the Lord for our salvation . . ."

Darkness, gradually lit up by dim candles before icons. Interior of a monastery church. The flickering light reveals a table where candles are sold, a wide bench near it, a latticed window, the chocolate-colored image of a saint, faded seraphs' wings, gold halos. Behind the window a cheerless October evening, snow and sleet. On the bench, completely covered by a horsecloth, lies BARABANCHIKOVA.

The chemist MAKHROV, *in a sheepskin coat, is peering out the window, trying to make out something.* SERAFIMA, *in a black fur coat, sits in the high chair of the Father Superior. Judging by her face, she is ill. At her feet on a low bench, next to a suitcase, sits* GOLUBKOV, *a young man of the St. Petersburg variety, in a black coat and in gloves.*

GOLUBKOV (*listening to the singing*): Do you hear, Serafima Vladimirovna? I thought they had an underground

vault . . . How strange it all is, really! Do you know,
at times it seems to me I'm dreaming! We've been
fleeing for a month now, Serafima Vladimirovna,
through villages and cities, and the farther we go, the
more incomprehensible it all becomes . . . And now
we're in this church! Do you know, in the midst of all
that uproar today, I suddenly felt homesick for Petersburg, I did! I had such a clear picture of the green-
shaded lamp in my study . . .

SERAFIMA: These moods are dangerous, Sergey Pavlovich.
Beware of feeling homesick when you are wandering.
Perhaps it would have been better if you had stayed
home?

GOLUBKOV: Oh, no, no, this is irrevocable, come what may!
And then, you know what makes this wretched journey
bearable for me . . . From the moment we met in that
freight car, under the lantern, you remember . . . actually, such a short time ago, but it seems to me I've
known you for years and years! The thought of you
brightens this flight through autumn darkness. I shall
be proud and happy when I bring you safely to the
Crimea and turn you over to your husband. And
though I shall miss you, I shall be happy in your
happiness. (SERAFIMA *silently puts her hand on Golubkov's shoulder. He strokes her hand.*) But wait, you
seem to have a fever?

SERAFIMA: No, it's nothing at all.

GOLUBKOV: What do you mean, nothing? You're feverish,
I'm sure you are!

SERAFIMA: Nonsense, Sergey Pavlovich, it will pass . . .

A *soft cannon thud in the distance.* BARABANCHIKOVA
stirs and moans. SERAFIMA *turns to her.*

Madame, you can't be left without help. One of us will try to get through to the village, there must be a midwife there.

GOLUBKOV: I'll go.

BARABANCHIKOVA *silently clutches him by the coattail.*

SERAFIMA: Why don't you want him to go, my dear?

BARABANCHIKOVA (*capriciously*): No . . . it isn't necessary.

SERAFIMA *and* GOLUBKOV *are puzzled.*

MAKHROV (*in an undertone, to* GOLUBKOV): Mysterious, a most mysterious character!

GOLUBKOV (*in a whisper*): You think that . . .

MAKHROV: I don't think anything, only . . . these are evil times, sir. No telling who will cross your path! Now this peculiar lady, stretched out in a church . . .

The singing below dies out.

PAISY (*appears soundlessly, black, frightened*): Your documents, prepare your documents, dear, honest folk! (*Blows out all the candles, except one.*)

SERAFIMA, GOLUBKOV *and* MAKHROV *take out their documents.* BARABANCHIKOVA *stretches her hand and puts her passport on the horsecloth that covers her.* BAYEV *enters in a short sheepskin coat sprayed with mud, excited. Followed by a* SOLDIER *of the Budenny army, carrying a lantern.*

BAYEV: The devil choke them, those monks! Ugh, a nest of vipers! Hey, holy pop, where's the staircase to the bell tower?

PAISY: Here, here, right here . . .

BAYEV (*to the* SOLDIER): Go take a look.

The SOLDIER *with the lantern disappears behind the iron door.*

(*To* PAISY.) Was there a light in the bell tower?

PAISY: What do you mean? What light?

BAYEV: There was a flickering light! Just wait, if I find anything in the bell tower, I'll line you up against the wall, to the last one of you, together with your gray old devil! Were you swinging lanterns?

PAISY: Heaven forbid! What are you saying?

BAYEV: And who are these? You've told me there wasn't an outside soul in the monastery!

PAISY: They're refugees, ref ...

SERAFIMA: We were caught by the fire in the village, Comrade, and we ran here, to the monastery. (*Points to* BARABANCHIKOVA.) This woman, she is going into labor ...

BAYEV (*walks over to* BARABANCHIKOVA, *picks up the passport, reads*): Barabanchikova, married ...

PAISY (*frenzied with terror, whispers*): Merciful Lord, save and protect us! (*Wants to run away.*) Holy martyr Dimitry ...

BAYEV: Where's her husband? (BARABANCHIKOVA *moans.*) Fine time and place to bear children! (*To* MAKHROV.) Your documents!

MAKHROV: Right here! I am a chemist from Mariupol.

BAYEV: Too many of you chemists hanging around here, along the front!

MAKHROV: I've come to buy some produce, cucumbers ...

BAYEV: Cucumbers!

SOLDIER (*reappears suddenly*): Comrade Bayev! I found nothing in the bell tower, but ... (*Whispers into Bayev's ear.*)

BAYEV: No! Where from?

SOLDIER: It's true, I tell you. The main thing, it's dark, Comrade Commander.

BAYEV: All right, all right, let's go. (*To* GOLUBKOV, *who holds out his documents.*) No time, no time now, later. (*To* PAISY.) So the monks are taking no sides in the civil war?

PAISÝ: No, no, no . . .

BAYEV: Just praying? And who're you praying for, I'd like to know? The Black Baron or the Soviet Government? All right, goodbye now, we'll see about everything tomorrow! (*Exits with* SOLDIER.)

Muffled sounds of a command outside, and everything is quiet again as though nothing has happened. PAISY *crosses himself again and again with quick, avid movements, relights the candles and disappears.*

MAKHROV: Gone . . . It is rightly said, "And he causeth them to receive a mark in their hands and in their foreheads . . ."* Those five-pointed stars, did you see?

GOLUBKOV (*whispers to* SERAFIMA): I can't understand it, this area is in White hands, where did the Reds come from? A surprise attack? . . . How did it happen?

BARABANCHIKOVA: It happened because General Krapchikov is an asshole, not a general! (*To* SERAFIMA.) My apologies, Madame.

GOLUBKOV (*mechanically*): Why?

BARABANCHIKOVA: That's why. They sent him a wire that the Red Cavalry was moving in behind him, and he— blast his soul!—he didn't bother to decode it . . . left it for the morning, and sat down to a game of vint.

---

* Rev. 13:16

GOLUBKOV: Oh? . . .

BARABANCHIKOVA: Declared a little slam in hearts.

MAKHROV (*quietly*): Oh, what an interesting character!

GOLUBKOV: Excuse me, but you seem to be informed. I had been told that General Charnota's headquarters were here, in Kurchulan . . .

BARABANCHIKOVA: Such detailed information! So they were, and now they're gone.

GOLUBKOV: But where?

BARABANCHIKOVA: Quite definitely . . . into the swamp.

MAKHROV: And how do you know all this, Madame?

BARABANCHIKOVA: You're much too curious, Your Eminence!

MAKHROV: Excuse me, but why do you address me as Your Eminence?

BARABANCHIKOVA: All right, all right, you bore me, get away from me.

PAISY *runs in, puts out all but one of the candles again, and looks out of the window.*

GOLUBKOV: What now?

PAISY: Oh, sir, we don't know ourselves whom the Lord may be sending us now, or whether we'll live through the night! (*Disappears so silently, it seems that he was swallowed by the earth.*)

The clatter of many hooves, lights flickering in the windows.

SERAFIMA: A fire?

GOLUBKOV: No, torches. I understand nothing, Serafima Vladimirovna! White troops, I swear they're White! It's come to pass! Serafima Vladimirovna, thank God, we are in the hands of Whites again! Officers with shoulder straps!

BARABANCHIKOVA (*sits up, wrapping herself in the horse-cloth*): You, blasted intellectual, shut up! "Shoulder straps, shoulder straps!" This isn't Petersburg, it's Tauria, a treacherous land! If someone pinned on shoulder straps, it doesn't mean that he's turned White. And if it's a disguised platoon? What then?

The church bell rings out suddenly, in muted tones.

Now they're ringing! Those idiot monks! (*To* GOLUB-KOV.) What color trousers?

GOLUBKOV: Red! . . . And now another unit is riding in, these have blue trousers with red sides . . .

BARABANCHIKOVA: "Riding in with sides!" The devil take you! Stripes?

The muffled sound of De Brizar's command, "First squadron, dismount!"

What's that? It can't be! His voice! (*To* GOLUBKOV.) Now you can shout, now you can shout at the top of your voice, I give you permission! (*Throws off the horsecloth and rags and leaps out as* GENERAL CHAR-NOTA. *He is wearing a Circassian coat with crumpled silver shoulder straps. Puts the revolver he had in his hand into his pocket, runs to the window, flings it open and shouts.*) Hussars! Don cavalry! Welcome! Colonel De Brizar, come in!

The door opens and LYUSKA *runs in first, wearing a nurse's triangular kerchief on her head, a leather jacket and high boots with spurs. She is followed by* DE BRI-ZAR, *his face covered with a new growth of beard, and by Charnota's orderly* KRAPILIN, *carrying a torch.*

LYUSKA: Grisha! Gri-gri! (*Throws her arms around him.*) I can't believe my eyes! Alive? You got away? (*Shouts through the window.*) Hey, Hussars! General Charnota got away from the Reds! (*Noise and shouts outside the window.*) We were going to say mass for you!

CHARNOTA: I've seen death as close as your kerchief. I come to Krapchikov's headquarters, and he makes me sit down to a game of vint, the son of a bitch . . . Little slam in hearts . . . and then—machine guns! Budenny dropping on our heads—out of the blue! Wiped out the whole headquarters! I shot my way out, jumped through the window, and cut across the backyards to the village, to Barabanchikov, the teacher. Give me your documents, I say! And he's so panicked, he hands me the wrong papers! I crept here, to the monastery, and gave a look—a woman's papers, Madame Barabanchikova's, and a certificate—she's pregnant! And the Reds are all around. All right, I say, let me stretch out, as I am, right here in church! I lie here, in labor, and I hear spurs—click, click! . . .

LYUSKA: Who?

CHARNOTA: An officer, Budenny's cavalry.

LYUSKA: Oh!

CHARNOTA: So I think to myself—where are you clicking to, Red officer? Don't you know your death is waiting for you under the horsecloth? Come on, lift it up, lift it up fast! You'll be buried with music! He took the passport, but he never lifted the cloth!

LYUSKA *squeals.* CHARNOTA *runs to the door and calls out, "A welcome to you, Cossack tribe! A welcome!" Shouts are heard outside.* LYUSKA *runs out after* CHARNOTA.

DE BRIZAR: Oh, well, I'll lift the cloth all right! May I be damned for a spotted devil if I don't hang someone in this monastery, just to celebrate! Who are these? Left

behind by the Reds in their rush? (*To* MAKHROV.) I
don't have to ask you for your documents. I can see
by your hair what kind of a bird you are! Krapilin,
bring over the light!

PAISY (*rushes in*): No, no, what are you saying? This is
His Eminence, Archbishop Africanus!

DE BRIZAR: Quit jabbering, you black-tailed goblin!

MAKHROV *throws off his hat and coat.* DE BRIZAR *peers
into his face.*

What's this? Your Eminence, it's really you! How did
you get here?

AFRICANUS: I came to Kurchulan to bless the Don Corps,
and I was caught here when the Reds attacked. Thank
God, the monks provided me with documents.

DE BRIZAR: The devil knows what's going on! (*To* SERA-
FIMA.) Your documents, woman!

SERAFIMA: I am the wife of the Vice-Minister of Trade. I
was delayed in Petersburg, and my husband is already
in the Crimea. I am going there to join him. Here are
my false documents, and this is my real passport. My
name is Korzukhina.

DE BRIZAR: Mille excuses, Madame! And you, civilian caterpillar, you're not the Attorney General by any chance?

GOLUBKOV: I am not a caterpillar, and certainly not the
Attorney General! I am the son of Golubkov, the fa-
mous idealist professor, and an assistant professor myself. I am fleeing from Petersburg to you, the Whites,
because it is impossible to work in Petersburg.

DE BRIZAR: Charmed! A Noah's ark!

*The iron trap door in the floor opens, and the aged
FATHER SUPERIOR climbs out, followed by the monks'
chorus carrying candles.*

FATHER SUPERIOR (*to* AFRICANUS): Your Eminence! (*To the monks.*) Brethren! It has been granted to us to save and preserve our Archbishop from the hands of the impious socialists!

The monks drape a mantle over the shoulders of the agitated AFRICANUS *and bring him his staff.*

Accept thy staff once more, our Shepherd, and lead thy flock . . .

AFRICANUS: "O God of hosts, look down from heaven and behold, and visit this vine; and the vineyard which thy right hand hath planted!"*

Monks break into chanting "Εἰς πολλὰ ἔτη δέσποτα!. ."†
CHARNOTA *appears in the doorway with* LYUSKA.

CHARNOTA: What's going on here, Holy Fathers, have you lost your wits? A fine time for ceremonies! Get along, choir! (*Gestures to them to leave.*)
AFRICANUS: Depart, brethren!

The FATHER SUPERIOR *and the monks descend underground.*

CHARNOTA (*to* AFRICANUS): Your Eminence, what's the idea of this sacred service now? We've got to clear out! The Reds are on our heels, we'll be trapped like rats! Budenny will drive us into the sea! The whole army's leaving! To the Crimea! Under Roman Khludov's wing!
AFRICANUS: All-merciful Lord, what is this? (*Snatches up his sheepskin coat.*) Do you have any carriages? (*Disappears.*)

---

* Ps. 80:14–15
† Unto eternity, O Lord!

CHARNOTA: Get me a map! Krapilin, a light! (*Studies the map.*) All roads are closed! We're finished!

LYUSKA: That Krapchikov, that Krapchikov!

CHARNOTA: Wait! I've found it! I've found an opening! (*To* DE BRIZAR.) Take your regiment and go toward Almanaika. You'll divert them for a while, then make it fast to Babi Guy and cross over, even if the water's up to your neck! I'll start out after you with the Don Cossacks, to the Molokan villages; we'll get to the Arbat Spur a bit later than you, but there we'll reunite. I give you five minutes to start!

DE BRIZAR: Yes, Your Excellency.

CHARNOTA: Uph! . . . let me have a sip, Colonel.

GOLUBKOV: Serafima Vladimirovna, do you hear? The Whites are leaving. We must go with them, or we'll fall into the hands of the Reds again. Serafima Vladimirovna, why don't you answer, what is it?

LYUSKA: Let me have some too.

DE BRIZAR *gives his flask to* LYUSKA.

GOLUBKOV (*to* CHARNOTA): General, I beg you, take us with you! Serafima Vladimirovna is ill . . . We are fleeing to the Crimea . . . Do you have a field hospital?

CHARNOTA: You've studied at the university?

GOLUBKOV: Of course, yes . . .

CHARNOTA: You strike me as a total ignoramus. Suppose you get a bullet in your brain at Babi Guy, what good will a field hospital do you? Why don't you ask if we have an X-ray laboratory? Intellectuals! . . . Give me another swig of cognac!

LYUSKA: We must take them. She's a beautiful woman, the Reds will get her . . .

GOLUBKOV: Serafima Vladimirovna, get up! We must go!

SERAFIMA (*tonelessly*): You know, Sergey Pavlovich, I

think I'm really sick. You go on by yourself, and I'll lie
down here, in the monastery . . . I feel so hot . . .

GOLUBKOV: Good God! Serafima Vladimirovna, it's unthinkable! Serafima Vladimirovna, stand up!

SERAFIMA: I want a drink . . . I want to go to Petersburg . . .

GOLUBKOV: What is this?

LYUSKA (*triumphantly*): It's typhus, that's what it is.

DE BRIZAR: Madame, you must escape, you'll have a bad
time with the Reds. But I'm not much of a talker.
Krapilin, you're the eloquent one, try to convince the
lady!

KRAPILIN: That's right, ma'am, you've got to come!

GOLUBKOV: Serafima Vladimirovna, we must go . . .

DE BRIZAR (*glancing at his wristwatch*): Time! (*Runs out.*)

*The sound of his command, "Mount!" and the clatter
of hooves.*

LYUSKA: Krapilin! Pick her up, make her come!

KRAPILIN: Yes, ma'am!

*KRAPILIN and GOLUBKOV lift SERAFIMA and lead her
under the arms.*

LYUSKA: Get her into a carriage!

Exeunt.

CHARNOTA (*alone, finishing up the cognac, looks at his
watch*): Time!

FATHER SUPERIOR (*rises through the trap door*): White
general! Where are you off to? Won't you defend the
monastery that gave you shelter and saved your life?

CHARNOTA: You're upsetting me, Father! Tie up the bells'
tongues and go underground! Goodbye! (*Disappears.*)

*His shout outside, "Mount!" Thunder of hooves, then
silence.* PAISY *appears through the trap door.*

PAISY: Father Superior! Father Superior! What shall we
do? The Reds will be here any moment! And we
rang for the Whites! Are we to suffer martyrdom?
FATHER SUPERIOR: But where is the Archbishop?
PAISY: Gone, galloped away in an army cart!
FATHER SUPERIOR: Unworthy, unworthy shepherd! Abandoned his flock! (*Cries in a muffled voice into the
vault.*) Pray, brethren!

*Muted sounds from underground, "Holy Saint Nicho-
las, pray to the Lord for our salvation . . ."*

Darkness swallows the monastery.

My dreams grow ever more troubled . . .

SECOND DREAM

*Out of the darkness emerges a waiting room in a large rail-
way station somewhere in northern Crimea. Extraordinarily
large windows in the back. Behind the windows, black
night with blue electric moons.*

*A beastly, incomprehensible frost, unusual for the beginning
of November, has struck the Crimea. It has paralyzed the
Sivash, Chongar, Perekop, and this station. The windows
are frosted over; snakelike, fiery reflections of passing
trains flow across the icy mirrors from time to time. Porta-
ble black iron stoves are burning in the room. Kerosene
lamps on the tables. Farther in, over the exit to the main
platform, there is a sign,* ARRIVALS AND DEPARTURES.

*A glass partition; behind it, a lamp with a green shade and
two green conductors' lanterns, like the eyes of some monster. Next to them an icon: against a dark, peeling background, a white youth on a horse, striking a scaly dragon
with his lance. The youth is St. George, and a varicolored,
faceted icon-lamp burns before him.*

*The waiting room is filled with White staff officers. Most
of them are wearing Caucasian cowls or earmuffs. Number-*

18

less field telephones, maps with pins and flags, typewriters in the background. Colored signal lights are constantly flashing on the telephones; telephones ring in delicate tones.

The station has served as the front headquarters for three days, and for three days it has not slept, working like a machine. And only an experienced and observant eye could catch the tinge of anxiety in the eyes of all these people, and the fear and hope that flickered there whenever they turn to what has once been the First Class bar.

There, divided from everyone by the high cabinet of the bar, ROMAN VALERIANOVICH KHLUDOV sits huddled on a high stool behind the counter. This man's face is white as a bone, his hair is black, with the eternal indestructible part favored by officers. He is pug-nosed like Emperor Paul I, clean-shaven like an actor, seems younger than everyone else, but his eyes are old. He is wearing a soldier's overcoat, loosely belted with a leather strap. His shoulder straps are made of cloth, with the general's zigzag insignia tacked on carelessly. His khaki cap is dirty, with a visor that has lost its shine. He wears mittens on his hands, and has no weapons of any kind.

Something ails this man, he is sick from head to foot. He wrinkles his face, twitches, is fond of changing his intonations. He asks himself questions, and answers them himself. When he wants to show a smile, he bares his teeth. He is frightening. He is sick.

On the table near Khludov there are several telephones. The Cossack captain, GOLOVAN, sits at the table, writing. He is a devoted secretary, and he worships KHLUDOV.

KHLUDOV (*dictating to* GOLOVAN): Comma. But Frunze refused to take the part of the enemy at maneuvers. Stop. This is not chess and not the unforgettable Tsarskoye Selo. Stop. Signed Khludov. Stop.

GOLOVAN (*hands the sheet to someone*): Code it and send it to the Commander in Chief.

FIRST STAFF OFFICER (*face lit up by the signal on his telephone; moans into it*): Yes, I'm listening . . . Yes . . . Budenny? Budenny?

SECOND STAFF OFFICER (*moans into his telephone*): Taganash . . . Taganash . . .

THIRD STAFF OFFICER (*moans into his telephone*): No, to the Karpov Ravine . . .

GOLOVAN (*lit up by signal, hands the receiver to* KHLUDOV): Your Excellency . . .

KHLUDOV (*into the receiver*): Yes. Yes. Yes. No. Yes. (*Returns receiver to* GOLOVAN.) Get the Commandant.

GOLOVAN: The Commandant!

A *running echo of voices:* "The Commandant, the Commandant!" *The station* COMMANDANT, *an officer in a red cap, pale, flustered, his eyes darting in all directions, hurries across the waiting room, among the tables, and comes before* KHLUDOV.

KHLUDOV: I've been waiting for the armored train to Taganash for an hour. What's wrong? What's wrong? What's wrong?

COMMANDANT (*in a dead voice*): The Stationmaster says the train cannot get through, Your Excellency, he proved it to me.

KHLUDOV: Get me the Stationmaster.

COMMANDANT (*speaks to someone in a sobbing voice as he runs*): What am I to do?

KHLUDOV: Our tragedies are starting. The armored train has been struck by paralysis. The armored train is hobbling with a cane, it cannot get through. (*Rings the bell.*)

A sign flashes on the wall, "Counter-intelligence Section." TIKHY seems to come out of the wall in response to Khludov's bell, stops near KHLUDOV, quiet and attentive.

(*To* TIKHY.) Nobody loves us, nobody. All our tragedies come from that, just like in the theater. (TIKHY *is silent. Furiously.*) Is the stove smoking? Is everybody felled by charcoal fumes?

GOLOVAN: No, there are no fumes.

The COMMANDANT *appears before* KHLUDOV, *followed by the* STATIONMASTER.

KHLUDOV (*to the* STATIONMASTER): You proved to him that the train cannot get through?

STATIONMASTER (*he speaks and moves, but he has been dead for the past twenty-four hours*): Yes, Sir, Your Excellency. It's physically impossible! All tracks are jammed!

KHLUDOV: So, another stove is smoking!

GOLOVAN: Just a moment! (*Shouts aside to someone.*) Put out the stove, pour water on it!

STATIONMASTER: Fumes, fumes.

KHLUDOV (*to the* STATIONMASTER): For some reason it seems to me that you like the Bolsheviks. Don't be afraid, you can talk to me openly. Every man has his convictions, and he should not conceal them. Sly fox!

STATIONMASTER (*babbles nonsense*): Your Excellency, how can you suspect me of such a thing? I have children

. . . Even at the time of the Emperor Nicholas Alexandrovich . . . Olya and Pavlik, little children . . . I haven't slept for thirty hours—God is my witness!—and I'm known personally to the chairman of the State Duma, Mikhail Vladimirovich Rodzyanko. But I don't sympathize with him, with Rodzyanko . . . I have little children . . .

KHLUDOV: A sincere man, eh? No? There must be love, without love you can't do anything in a war! (*Reproachfully, to* TIKHY.) I am not loved. (*Drily.*) Get the sappers. Push the cars! Clear the tracks! I give you fifteen minutes to get the train past the semaphore! If my order is not carried out by then, arrest the Commandant! And hang the Stationmaster on the semaphore, with a lighted sign under him, "Sabotage."

A delicate, slow waltz is heard in the distance. Once upon a time this waltz was played at school dances.

STATIONMASTER (*dully*): Your Excellency, my children have not started school yet . . .

TIKHY *takes the* STATIONMASTER *by the elbow and leads him away. The* COMMANDANT *follows them.*

KHLUDOV: A waltz?

GOLOVAN: Charnota is coming, Your Excellency.

STATIONMASTER (*behind the glass partition, revives and shouts into the telephone*): Khristophor Fyodorovich! I beg you, in the name of God Almighty! Rush all trains from the fourth and fifth tracks straight to Taganash! You'll have sappers! Anyway you wish, but rush them out! For God's sake!

NIKOLAYEVNA *appears near the* STATIONMASTER.

NIKOLAYEVNA: What is it, Vasya? What is it?

STATIONMASTER: Oh, we're in trouble, Nikolayevna! Our family's in trouble! Get Olka, bring her here just as she is, bring Olka!

NIKOLAYEVNA: Olka? Olka? (*Disappears.*)

The waltz breaks off. The door from the platform opens and CHARNOTA *enters, in cloak and Cossack fur hat. He walks through to* KHLUDOV. LYUSKA, *who ran in with him, remains by the door in the background.*

CHARNOTA: From the Chongar defile, Your Excellency, composite cavalry division. (KHLUDOV *looks at* CHARNOTA *in silence.*) Your Excellency! (*Points somewhere outside into the distance.*) What are you doing? (*Suddenly removes his hat.*) Roma! You're a member of the General Staff! What are you doing? You must stop it, Roma!

KHLUDOV: Silence! (CHARNOTA *puts on his hat.*) Leave the transport here. Go to Karpov Ravine, take a stand there.

CHARNOTA: Yes, Sir. (*Walks away.*)

LYUSKA: Where?

CHARNOTA (*bleakly*): The Karpov Ravine.

LYUSKA: I'm going with you. I'm leaving those wounded men and the sick Serafima!

CHARNOTA (*bleakly*): You may get killed.

LYUSKA: Then thanks be to the Lord! (*Leaves with him.*)

Clanking and clattering outside, then the agonized howl of the armored train. NIKOLAYEVNA *bursts in from behind the partition, dragging* OLKA, *wrapped in a shawl.*

NIKOLAYEVNA: Here she is, here is Olka!

STATIONMASTER (*into a telephone*): Khristophor Fyodoro-vich, you brought it in? Thank you, thank you!

Picks up OLKA *and runs to* KHLUDOV. *He is followed by* TIKHY *and the* COMMANDANT.

KHLUDOV (*to the* STATIONMASTER): Well, my good man, so it got through? It got through?

STATIONMASTER: It got through, Your Excellency, it got through!

KHLUDOV: And what's the child for?

STATIONMASTER: It's Olechka, my baby . . . a clever child. I've been on this job for twenty years. I haven't slept two nights in a row.

KHLUDOV: Yes, a girl . . . A hoop. Does she play with a hoop? Yes? (*Takes a caramel from his pocket.*) Here, girl! The doctors say I mustn't smoke, my nerves are shot. But the caramels don't help, I smoke and smoke anyway.

STATIONMASTER: Take it, Olyushka, take it . . . The general is kind. Say merci, Olyushka . . . (*Picks her up and carries her away behind the partition.* NIKOLAYEVNA *and* OLKA *disappear.*)

The waltz is heard again, and begins to recede into the distance. PARAMON ILYICH KORZUKHIN *enters, not through the door used by Charnota, but through another one. He is a man of European appearance, wearing glasses, in a very expensive fur coat, carrying a briefcase. He approaches* GOLOVAN *and offers him his calling card, who gives it to* KHLUDOV.

KHLUDOV: I'm listening.

KORZUKHIN (*to* KHLUDOV): Permit me to introduce myself.

Vice-Minister of Trade, Korzukhin. The Council of Ministers has delegated me, Your Excellency, to address three inquiries to you. I have just come from Sebastopol. First: I was asked to inquire about the fate of the five workers arrested in Simferopol and brought here, to your headquarters, at your command.

KHLUDOV: So. Ah, yes, you came from the other platform! Captain! Present the prisoners to the Vice-Minister.

GOLOVAN: Follow me, please.

While everyone watches tensely, he conducts KOR- ZUKHIN *to the main door in the back of the waiting room, opens it slightly and points up.* KORZUKHIN *starts. They return to* KHLUDOV.

KHLUDOV: Is the first question answered? I'm listening to the second.

KORZUKHIN (*nervously*): The second has to do directly with my Ministry. Some extremely important freight has been held up at this station. I want to beg your permission and aid in getting it through immediately to Sebastopol.

KHLUDOV (*gently*): And what precisely does this freight consist of?

KORZUKHIN: Furs for export, for delivery abroad.

KHLUDOV (*with a smile*): Ah, furs, for export! And which trains contain this freight?

KORZUKHIN (*hands him a paper*): Here, if you please.

KHLUDOV: Captain Golovan! Have the trains indicated here taken to a dead rail and burned! Use kerosene! (GOLOVAN *takes the paper and disappears.* KHLUDOV, *gently.*) And now, briefly, your third question?

KORZUKHIN (*stunned*): The situation at the front? . . .

KHLUDOV (*yawns*): Well, what can the situation be at the

front! Total confusion! They're firing cannons. They've
set a smoking stove under the front commander's nose.
The Commander in Chief sent me some Cubans as
a present, and they're barefoot. No restaurant, no girls!
You die of green boredom. And so we're sitting here
on stools, like parrots. (*Changes his intonation to a
hiss.*) The situation? Go to Sebastopol, Monsieur
Korzukhin, and tell the civilian lice to pack their bags!
The Reds will be here tomorrow! And also tell them
that the foreign whores will get along without sable
cuffs! Furs!

KORZUKHIN: It's unheard-of! (*Looks around like an animal
at bay.*) I shall have the honor of reporting this to the
Commander in Chief.

KHLUDOV (*politely*): Certainly.

KORZUKHIN (*backs away to a side door, asking as he moves*):
When's the next train to Sebastopol?

No one answers him. A train is heard coming in.

STATIONMASTER (*appears before* KHLUDOV, *numb with
terror*): Special from Kerman Kemalchi!

KHLUDOV: Attention, officers!

*Everybody gets up. In the door through which Kor-
zukhin has just left appear two Cossack guards in
crimson cowls. They are followed by the* COMMANDER
IN CHIEF OF THE WHITE ARMIES, *in a Cossack fur hat
pushed smartly back, a long coat, and a Caucasian
sword; behind him, His Eminence* AFRICANUS, *blessing
the headquarters.*

COMMANDER IN CHIEF: Good evening, gentlemen!

STAFF OFFICERS: Good evening, Your Excellency.

KHLUDOV: I beg permission to report to Your Excellency
in private.

COMMANDER IN CHIEF: Yes. Everyone leave the room. (*To* AFRICANUS.) Archbishop, I shall speak to the Commander of the Front in private.

AFRICANUS: In a blessed hour! In a blessed hour!

Everyone leaves, and KHLUDOV *remains alone with the* COMMANDER IN CHIEF.

KHLUDOV: Three hours ago the enemy took Yushun. The Bolsheviks are in the Crimea.

COMMANDER IN CHIEF: The end?

KHLUDOV: The end.

Silence.

COMMANDER IN CHIEF (*speaks through the door*): Your Eminence!

AFRICANUS *enters. He looks alarmed.*

Your Eminence! Abandoned by the Western Powers, deceived by the faithless Poles, our only hope at this black hour is in Divine Mercy!

AFRICANUS (*realizes the gravity of the situation*): Oh! Oh!

COMMANDER IN CHIEF: Pray, Holy Father!

AFRICANUS (*before St. George*): Almighty Lord! Why? Why dost Thou visit this new ordeal upon Thy sons, the glorious army of Christ? The power of the Cross is with us, it overthrows the foe with blessed arms . . .

The face of the STATIONMASTER, *sick with fear, appears behind the glass partition.*

KHLUDOV: Forgive the interruption, Your Eminence, but you're troubling the good Lord for nothing. He has long abandoned us, that is clear. Just look around you. Has such a thing ever happened before? The waters of the Sivash were turned away, and the Bolsheviks crossed over as on a parquet floor. St. George is laughing!

AFRICANUS: What are you saying, General!

COMMANDER IN CHIEF: I absolutely protest against such a tone. You're obviously sick, General, I'm sorry you didn't go abroad for a cure last summer, as I advised you.

KHLUDOV: Ah, I see! And who would have gotten your soldiers to hold the forts for you at Perekop, Your Excellency? Who would have sent off Charnota this night, with music, straight from Chongar to the Karpov Ravine? And the hangings? Who would have done the hangings, Your Excellency?

COMMANDER IN CHIEF (*his face darkening*): What's this?

AFRICANUS: Look down upon them, Lord, enlighten and fortify them! For "Every kingdom divided against itself is brought to desolation!"*

COMMANDER IN CHIEF: However, this is not the time . . .

KHLUDOV: No, this isn't the time. You must return to Sebastopol without delay.

COMMANDER IN CHIEF: You're right. (*Takes out an envelope and gives it to* KHLUDOV.) Please open it at once.

KHLUDOV: Ah, you have it ready! You foresaw this? Good. "Lord, now lettest thou thy servant depart in peace . . ."† Yes, Sir. (*Shouts.*) A train for the Commander in Chief! Convoy! Staff!

STATIONMASTER (*rushes to the telephone behind the partition*): Kerman Kemalchi! A train! Give the signal, the signal!

The Cossack convoy and the STAFF OFFICERS *appear.*

---

* Matt. 12:25
† Luke 2:29

COMMANDER IN CHIEF: The Commander of the Front . . . (*The officers salute.*) . . . will read my orders to you! May the Lord send you all strength and wisdom to live through the evil days in Russia! I frankly warn each and every one of you that the Crimea is all we have.

The door bursts open suddenly and DE BRIZAR *appears, head wrapped in bandages, and salutes the* COMMANDER IN CHIEF.

DE BRIZAR: Long life to Your Imperial Majesty! (*To the* STAFF OFFICERS, *mysteriously.*) "Countess, for a single rendezvous I shall be glad to name to you . . ."*

COMMANDER IN CHIEF: What's this?

GOLOVAN: Commander of a Hussar Regiment, Count de Brizar. He has a head wound.

KHLUDOV (*as though asleep*): Chongar . . . Chongar . . .

COMMANDER IN CHIEF: Get him into my train, I'll take him with me to Sebastopol! (*Walks out rapidly, accompanied by his Cossack convoy.*)

AFRICANUS: Lord! Lord! (*Blesses the headquarters, walks out rapidly.*)

DE BRIZAR (*as he is led out by* STAFF OFFICERS): Pardon! . . . "Countess, for a single rendezvous . . ."

STAFF OFFICERS: To Sebastopol, Count, to Sebastopol . . .

DE BRIZAR: Pardon! . . . Pardon . . . (*Disappears.*)

KHLUDOV (*opens the envelope, reads. Bares his teeth. To* GOLOVAN): Send off a courier to the Karpov Ravine to General Barbovich. Orders are to break from the enemy, gallop to Yalta and embark!

---

* From *The Queen of Spades*, the Tchaikovsky opera based on a story by Alexander Pushkin.

A *rustling of whispers throughout headquarters,*
"Amen, Amen . . ." Then graveyard silence.

Another—to General Kutepov: break away, rush to
Sebastopol, embark. Fostikov and the Cubans—to
Theodosia. Kalinin and the Don Cossacks—to Kerch.
Charnota—to Sebastopol! Everyone to embark! Close
headquarters immediately, to Sebastopol! The Crimea
is surrendered!

GOLOVAN (*exits hastily*): Couriers! Couriers!

The groups of STAFF OFFICERS *begin to melt away.*
Maps are rolled up, telephones disappear. Outside, a
train whistle howls and the trains pull out. Confusion,
all order gone. The door through which CHARNOTA
had left bursts open and SERAFIMA *appears, wearing a*
Cossack cloak. She is followed by GOLUBKOV *and*
KRAPILIN, *who try to restrain her.*

GOLUBKOV: Serafima Vladimirovna, think what you're doing, you must not go in! (*To the astonished* STAFF
OFFICERS.) She's sick, typhus! . . .

KRAPILIN: Yes, typhus.

SERAFIMA (*in a ringing voice*): Which one is Roman
Khludov?

A silence falls in response to the absurd question.

KHLUDOV: It's all right, let her in. I am Khludov.

GOLUBKOV: Don't listen to her, she is sick!

SERAFIMA: We are running from Petersburg, running and
running . . . Where? To safety under Khludov's wing!
All you hear is Khludov and Khludov . . . You even
dream about Khludov! (*Smiles.*) And now I have the
honor of beholding him: he sits on a stool, and all

around him, hanging bags. Bags and bags! . . . Beast!
Jackal!

GOLUBKOV (*desperately*): She has typhus! She is delirious!
. . . We're from the transport!

KHLUDOV *rings.* TIKHY *and* GURIN *emerge from the wall.*

SERAFIMA: Oh, well! They're coming, they'll finish you off!

The STAFF OFFICERS *whisper,* "A-ah, a Communist!"

GOLUBKOV: Oh, no! Oh, no! She is the wife of the Vice-
Minister of Trade, Korzukhin! She doesn't know what
she's saying!

KHLUDOV: That's good. Our people, when they know what
they're saying, will never say a word of truth.

GOLUBKOV: She is Korzukhina!

KHLUDOV: Wait, wait, wait! Korzukhina? Export fur? So the
scoundrel has a Communist wife, too? O-oh, blessed
occasion! Well, I'll take care of him! Bring him in, if
he hasn't run off yet!

TIKHY *signals to* GURIN, *and he disappears.*

TIKHY (*gently, to* SERAFIMA): What is your name and
patronymic, please?

GOLUBKOV: Serafima Vladimirovna . . . Serafima . . .

GURIN *brings in* KORZUKHIN. *He is deathly pale, sensing
trouble.*

Are you Paramon Ilyich Korzukhin?

KORZUKHIN: Yes, I am.

GOLUBKOV: Thank God, you've come to meet us! At last!

TIKHY (*in caressing tones, to* KORZUKHIN): Your wife,
Serafima Vladimirovna, has come to you from Petersburg.

KORZUKHIN (*looks* TIKHY *and* KHLUDOV *in the eyes, senses a trap*): I don't know any Serafima Vladimirovna, I see this woman for the first time in my life, I'm not expecting anyone from Petersburg, it's a lie.

SERAFIMA (*with a blurred look at* KORZUKHIN): A-ah, you disown me! Ugh, vermin!

KORZUKHIN: It's blackmail!

GOLUBKOV (*frantically*): Paramon Ilyich, what are you doing? This isn't possible!

KHLUDOV: A sincere man, eh? Your luck, Monsieur Korzukhin! Furs! Out!

KORZUKHIN *vanishes.*

GOLUBKOV: I beg you to interrogate us! I shall prove she is his wife!

KHLUDOV (*to* TIKHY): Take them both, interrogate them!

TIKHY (*to* GURIN): Take them to Sebastopol.

GURIN *takes* SERAFIMA *by the elbow.*

GOLUBKOV: You are intelligent people! . . . I shall prove . . .

SERAFIMA: There, a single decent man on the way . . . Ah, Krapilin, eloquent man, why don't you speak up for us?

SERAFIMA *and* GOLUBKOV *are led away.*

KRAPILIN (*confronts* KHLUDOV): That's right. Just as the books say, a jackal! But you can't win the war with rope alone! Why did you butcher the soldiers at Perekop, beast? But one human being did come your way, a woman. She took pity on the strangled ones, that's all. But nobody can get past you, nobody! Right away you grab him, and into a bag! Do you feed on carrion?

TIKHY: May I take him away, Your Excellency?

KHLUDOV: No. There is a glimmering of sound sense about the war in his words. Talk, soldier, talk.

TIKHY *beckons to someone, and two counter-intelligence men come out of the door of the counter-intelligence office.* TIKHY *whispers, "Get a board." A third counter-intelligence man comes in, carrying a piece of plywood.*

KHLUDOV: What's your name, soldier?

KRAPILIN (*carried away to reckless heights*): A name, what's the difference? It's a name nobody knows—Krapilin, an orderly! But you will perish, jackal, you'll perish, wild beast, in a ditch! Just wait a while longer on your stool! (*Smiles.*) But no, you'll run, you'll run to Constantinople! You're only brave to hang women and locksmiths!

KHLUDOV: You are wrong, soldier, I've gone to the Chongar Road with music, and was wounded twice on the Road.

KRAPILIN: All the provinces spit on your music! (*Suddenly recollects himself, starts, drops to his knees, and pleads in a pitiful voice.*) Your Excellency, be merciful to Krapilin! I was raving!

KHLUDOV: No! You're a poor soldier! You began well, but the end was rotten. Groveling at my feet! Hang him! I can't bear the sight of him!

The counter-intelligence men instantly throw a black bag over Krapilin's head and drag him outside.

GOLOVAN (*appears*): Your Excellency's order is carried out. The couriers are on the way.

KHLUDOV: Everyone into the train, gentlemen. Captain, get my convoy ready and prepare a car!

Everyone disappears except KHLUDOV; *alone, he picks up the telephone and speaks.*

The Commander of the Front speaking. Order the armored train to go as far as it can get along the line, and fire, fire! Fire at Taganash, fire! Smash them into the ground—give them a parting present! Then have them blow up the tracks behind it and on to Sebastopol! (*Puts down the receiver. Sits alone, crumpled on the stool. The distant howl of the armored train.*) What is this sickness? Am I sick?

A blast of gunfire from the armored train. It is so heavy that the sound is almost unheard, but the electricity goes out instantly and the ice-crusted windows shatter. Now the platform becomes visible. Pale-blue electric lights. Under the first, on an iron post, hangs a long black bag; beneath it is the plywood board with a charcoal inscription, "Orderly Krapilin—a Bolshevik." Under the next light, another bag. Nothing is visible beyond.

(*Alone in the dusk, looks at the hanged* KRAPILIN.) I am sick, sick. But I don't know what ails me.

OLKA *appears in the dusk, lost sight of in the panic. She creeps along the floor in felt boots.*

STATIONMASTER (*looks for her and mumbles sleepily*): That fool, that fool, Nikolayevna . . . Olka, where is Olka? Olechka, Olya, where are you, silly, where are you going? (*Catches her and picks her up in his arms.*) Come, come to your father . . . Don't look there . . . (*Happy that he was not noticed, he vanishes into the darkness.*)

Act Two

A needle glows in a dream ...

THIRD DREAM

A melancholy light. Autumn twilight. Office of the Counter-Intelligence Section in Sebastopol. One window, a desk, a sofa. A pile of newspapers on a small table in the corner. A cabinet. Draperies. TIKHY *sits at the desk in civilian clothes. The door opens and* GURIN *admits* GOLUBKOV.

GURIN: Here ... (*Disappears.*)

TIKHY: Sit down, please.

GOLUBKOV (*in his coat, hat in hand*): Thank you. (*Sits down.*)

TIKHY: You seem to be an educated man? (GOLUBKOV *coughs timidly.*) And I am sure you realize how important it is for us, and, hence, for the command, to know the truth. The Reds are spreading nasty rumors about our counter-intelligence. In reality, this organization is carrying out a most difficult, and an entirely honorable, task of guarding the country against the Bolsheviks. Do you agree with me?

GOLUBKOV: Well, you see, I ...

TIKHY: Are you afraid of me?

GOLUBKOV: Yes.

TIKHY: But why? Have we done you any harm on the way here to Sebastopol?

GOLUBKOV: Oh, no, no, I couldn't say that!

TIKHY: Cigarette? (*Offers him cigarettes.*)

GOLUBKOV: I don't smoke, thank you. I beg you, tell me how she is!

TIKHY: Who is it that interests you?

GOLUBKOV: She . . . Serafima Vladimirovna, she was arrested together with me. I swear, it's simply an absurd misunderstanding! She had an attack, she is very ill!

TIKHY: You're excited, calm down. I shall tell you about her later. (*Silence.*) All right, you can quit playing the assistant professor! I'm fed up with this comedy! Swine! You dare to sit before me? Up! Attention!

GOLUBKOV (*getting up*): Oh, God!

TIKHY: You there, what's your real name?

GOLUBKOV: But . . . but . . . that's my real name, Golubkov!

TIKHY *takes out his revolver and aims it at* GOLUBKOV, *who covers his face with his hands.*

TIKHY: You don't seem to realize that you're in my hands, do you? Nobody'll come to help you here! Understand?

GOLUBKOV: I understand.

TIKHY: Fine, we'll make an agreement: you will tell me nothing but the truth. Look here. If you begin to lie, I will switch on this needle (*switches on the needle, which begins to glow with the heat*), and give you a taste of it. (*Turns off the needle.*)

GOLUBKOV: I swear to you, I am really . . .

TIKHY: Silence! You'll speak only when questioned. (*Puts away the revolver, picks up a pen, and speaks in a bored voice.*) Sit down, please. Your name, patronymic, and surname?

GOLUBKOV: Sergey Pavlovich Golubkov.

TIKHY (*writes with a bored air*): Your permanent residence?

GOLUBKOV: Petersburg.

TIKHY: Why did you come from Soviet Russia to the zone held by the Whites?

GOLUBKOV: I have long wanted to go to the Crimea. Conditions in Petersburg made it impossible for me to work. And then I met Serafima Vladimirovna on the train. She was also escaping, and we traveled together to join the Whites.

TIKHY: And why did the woman who calls herself Serafima Korzukhina come to White territory?

GOLUBKOV: I firmly . . . I know that she is really Serafima Korzukhina!

TIKHY: Korzukhin denied this at the station in your presence.

GOLUBKOV: I swear to you he lied!

TIKHY: Why should he lie?

GOLUBKOV: He was frightened, he felt he was threatened by some danger.

TIKHY *puts down his pen and moves his hand toward the needle.*

What are you doing? I'm telling you the truth!

TIKHY: Your nerves are shot, Mr. Golubkov. I am taking down your testimony, as you see, nothing else. How long has she been a member of the Communist Party?

GOLUBKOV: But that's impossible!

TIKHY: So. (*Moves the sheet of paper over to* GOLUBKOV *and gives him the pen.*) Write down everything you have just told me. I will dictate to you, to make it easier. I warn you, if you stop, I'll give you the needle. If you don't stop, you have nothing to fear. (*Switches on the needle, which casts its glow on the paper, and dictates.*) "I, Sergey Pavlovich Golubkov . . . (GOLUB-KOV *begins to write.*) have testified during interrogation at the Counter-Intelligence Section of the General Headquarters of the Comfront, on October 31, 1920, colon, Serafima Vladimirovna Korzukhina, wife of Paramon Ilyich Korzukhin . . ."—Don't stop!—"a member of the Communist Party, has come from the city of Petersburg to the area occupied by the Southern Russian Armed Forces to conduct Communist propaganda and establish contact with the underground in the city of Sebastopol, period. Assistant Professor . . . Signature." (*Takes the sheet of paper from* GOLUBKOV, *turns off the needle.*) Thank you for your sincere testimony, Mr. Golubkov. I am entirely convinced of your innocence. Forgive me if I was occasionally somewhat sharp with you. You are free. (*Rings.*)

GURIN (*enters*): Yes, Sir!

TIKHY: Take this prisoner out into the street and let him go, he is free.

GURIN (*to* GOLUBKOV): Come on.

GOLUBKOV *exits with* GURIN, *forgetting his hat.*

TIKHY: Lieutenant Skunsky!

SKUNSKY *enters. He is very gloomy.* TIKHY *turns on the lamp on the desk.*

Price this document! How much will Korzukhin pay to buy himself off?

SKUNSKY: Here, right at the gangway? Ten thousand dollars. In Constantinople it would be less. I advise you to get a confession from Korzukhina.

TIKHY: Right. Find some pretext to delay Korzukhin's embarkation for half an hour or so.

SKUNSKY: My share? (TIKHY *indicates with his fingers—two.*) I'll send the agents at once. Hurry up with Korzukhina. It's late, the cavalry is just about to embark. (*Exits.*)

TIKHY *rings.* GURIN *enters.*

TIKHY: Prisoner Korzukhina. Is she conscious?
GURIN: Seems a bit better now.
TIKHY: Let's have her.

GURIN *leaves and returns a little later, bringing* SERAFIMA. *She is feverish.* GURIN *exits.*

You are ill? I won't detain you, sit down on the sofa, please, over there, there.

SERAFIMA *sits down on the sofa.*

Confess that you came here for propaganda, and I will let you go.
SERAFIMA: What? What propaganda? Good God, why did I come here?

A *waltz is heard, it comes nearer, and with it, the clatter of hooves outside the window.*

Why are they playing a waltz here?
TIKHY: Charnota's cavalry is marching to the harbor. Let's not divert ourselves. Your confederate, Golubkov, has testified that you came here to conduct propaganda.
SERAFIMA (*lies down on sofa, breathing heavily*): Go away, everybody, leave the room, let me sleep . . .
TIKHY: No, pull yourself together. Read this. (*Shows Golubkov's testimony to* SERAFIMA.)
SERAFIMA (*squints, reads*): Petersburg . . . lamp . . . he's gone mad . . . (*Seizes the paper, crumples it, runs to the window, knocks out the pane with her elbow,*

and screams.) Help! Help! They're committing **a** crime here! Charnota! Here! Help!

TIKHY: Gurin!

GURIN *runs in, seizes* SERAFIMA.

Take the document from her! Ah, damn you!

The waltz breaks off. A face in a Cossack hat is seen for a moment in the window. A voice, "What's going on here?" Voices, slamming of doors, noise. The door opens and CHARNOTA *appears, in a Cossack cloak. Behind him are two men in cloaks.* SKUNSKY *comes running in.* GURIN *releases his hold of* SERAFIMA.

SERAFIMA: Charnota! Is it you? Charnota! Protect me! Look what they are doing to me! Look what they forced him to write!

CHARNOTA *takes the paper.*

TIKHY: I insist you leave the counter-intelligence office at once!

CHARNOTA: Oh, no, why leave? What are you doing with this woman?

TIKHY: Lieutenant Skunsky, call the guards!

CHARNOTA: I'll show you, guards! (*Pulls out his revolver.*) What are you doing to the woman?

TIKHY: Lieutenant Skunsky, put out the light! (*The light goes out. In the dark.*) You'll pay dearly for this, General Charnota!

Darkness.

*And a mixed multitude went up also with them ...**

FOURTH DREAM

Twilight. Study in a palace in Sebastopol. The study is in an extraordinary state: one of the draperies over the window is partly torn down; a whitish square on the wall marks the spot where the large war map had been. A wooden case on the floor, apparently filled with papers. The fireplace is burning. DE BRIZAR *sits motionless before it, with a bandaged head. The* COMMANDER IN CHIEF *enters.*

COMMANDER IN CHIEF: Well, how is your head?

DE BRIZAR: It doesn't hurt, Your Excellency. The doctor gave me pyramidon.

COMMANDER IN CHIEF: So. Pyramidon? (*Absent-mindedly.*) What do you think, do I look like Alexander of Macedon?

DE BRIZAR (*without surprise*): I haven't seen any portraits of His Majesty for a long time, Your Excellency.

COMMANDER IN CHIEF: Who are you talking about?

DE BRIZAR: Alexander of Macedon, Your Excellency.

COMMANDER IN CHIEF: His Majesty? . . . Hmm . . . Look here, Colonel, you need a rest. I was glad to give you

* Exod. 12:38

41

shelter in the palace, you've done your duty to your country. Now you must go, it's time.

DE BRIZAR: Where to, Your Excellency?

COMMANDER IN CHIEF: Board the ship. I'll take care of you abroad.

DE BRIZAR: Yes, Sir. When victory over the Reds is won, I shall be happy to be the first to salute you in the Kremlin!

COMMANDER IN CHIEF: Colonel, there's no need to put things so sharply. You think in extremes. Very well now. You will start out at once.

DE BRIZAR: Yes, Sir, Your Excellency. (*Walks to the door, stops, and sings with a mysterious air.*) "Countess, for a single rendezvous . . ." (*Disappears.*)

COMMANDER IN CHIEF (*speaks through the door*): Admit the remaining visitors regularly every three minutes, one after the other. I will see as many people as I can manage. Send a Cossack to escort Colonel de Brizar to my ship! Write a note to the doctor aboard that pyramidon is not a cure! He is obviously unhinged! (*Returns to the fireplace, muses.*) Alexander of Macedon . . . The scoundrels!

KORZUKHIN *enters.*

Yes?

KORZUKHIN: Vice-Minister Korzukhin.

COMMANDER IN CHIEF: Ah! Just in time! I meant to call you here, despite all this scramble. Monsieur Korzukhin, do I look like Alexander of Macedon? (KORZUKHIN *is taken aback.*) I am asking you seriously, do I look like him? (*Snatches a newspaper from the mantel and thrusts it at* KORZUKHIN.) You are the editor of this newspaper, aren't you? Then you're responsible for everything printed in it? This is your name, isn't it? Editor—Korzukhin! (*Reads.*) "The Commander in Chief paces the railway platform like Alexander of Macedon . . ." What's the meaning of this rot? Were there railway platforms at the time of Alexander of Macedon? And do I look like him? And this (*Reads.*) "One glance at his jolly face, and the worm of doubt must dissipate . . ." A worm is not a cloud, it cannot dissipate! And am I jolly? Very jolly, am I? Where did you find this mercenary horde of illiterates? How did you dare to print this shameful twaddle two days before the catastrophe? I shall bring you to trial in Constantinople! If you have a headache, take pyramidon!

The telephone bursts into loud ringing in the next room. The COMMANDER IN CHIEF *walks out, slamming the door.*

KORZUKHIN (*puffs, catches his breath*): Serves you right, Paramon Ilyich! What devil, I ask you, drove you to the palace? To complain to one raving maniac against another? All right, so they got Serafima Vladimirovna—what can I do? So she'll die—may she rest in the Heavenly Kingdom! Am I to lose my own life over her? Alexander of Macedon is a boor! . . . Bring me to trial? Excuse me, Paris is not Sebastopol! To Paris, then! And may you all be damned forever, and to the end of days! (*Rushes to the door.*)

AFRICANUS (*entering*): Amen. Mr. Korzukhin, the things that go on, eh?

KORZUKHIN: Yes, yes, yes . . . (*Slips out.*)

AFRICANUS (*looking at the cases*): Oh, Lord! Oh, Lord! "And the children of Israel journeyed from Rameses to Succoth, about six hundred thousand on foot that were men, beside children" Ah, ah . . . "And a mixed multitude went up also with them . . ."*

KHLUDOV *walks in rapidly.*

You, Your Excellency? And just a moment ago Mr. Korzukhin was here, how strange . . .

KHLUDOV: Was it you who sent me a Bible at Headquarters?

AFRICANUS: Of course, of course . . .

KHLUDOV: I remember. I read it in the train at night out of boredom. "Thou didst blow with thy wind, the sea covered them: they sank as lead in the mighty waters."† Of whom was this said? Huh? "I will pursue, I will overtake, I will divide the spoil; my lust shall be satisfied upon them; I will draw my sword, my hand shall destroy them."‡ How is that for memory? And he maligns me, he says I am mad! But what are *you* hanging around here for?

AFRICANUS: Hanging around! Roman Valerianovich! I am waiting for the Commander in Chief . . .

KHLUDOV: All things shall come to him who waits. Sounds like your Bible, doesn't it? Do you know what you'll get for your waiting?

AFRICANUS: What?

KHLUDOV: The Reds.

AFRICANUS: But can it be so soon?

KHLUDOV: Everything can be. We're sitting around here, quoting the Holy Writ, and at this very moment —just imagine!—the cavalry is trotting over from the

---

* Exod. 12:37
† Exod. 15:10
‡ Exod. 15:9

north to Sebastopol . . . (*Takes* AFRICANUS *to the window*). Look . . .

AFRICANUS: Half the sky's on fire! Merciful Lord!

KHLUDOV: That's it. You'd better hurry to the ship, saintly Father, to the ship!

AFRICANUS *crosses himself rapidly and leaves.*

Gone!

COMMANDER IN CHIEF (*enters*): Ah, thank God! I've been waiting for you impatiently. Well, did everyone get through?

KHLUDOV: The Greens gave the cavalry a rough time on the way.* On the whole, you may say they got through. As for me, I traveled in comfort. Huddled up in the corner of the compartment—I didn't bother anybody, and nobody bothered me. In short, murk, Your Excellency, as in the kitchen.

COMMANDER IN CHIEF: I don't quite understand you, what do you mean?

KHLUDOV: Oh, this happened when I was a child. I stepped into the kitchen once, at twilight—cockroaches all over the stove. I lit a match— ch-r-k—and they scurried off in all directions. The match went out. And again nothing but the rustling of their feet—shur-shur, murmur . . . That's how it is with us now—murk and rustling. I look and I think—where are they running? Like roaches—straight into a pail of water. Down from the kitchen table and—plop!

COMMANDER IN CHIEF: I thank you, General, for all you have done for the Crimea, with your great military gifts. I

---

* The Greens were anarchist peasant bands led by Makhno, who fought both the Whites and the Reds.

shall not detain you any longer. I am moving to a hotel myself.

KHLUDOV: Closer to the water?

COMMANDER IN CHIEF: If you do not stop forgetting yourself, I shall have you arrested.

KHLUDOV: I expected this. My escort is in the anteroom. There will be a great scandal—I am popular.

COMMANDER IN CHIEF: No, this is not sickness. For a whole year you've been camouflaging your hatred of me with revolting buffoonery.

KHLUDOV: I won't deny it, I hate you.

COMMANDER IN CHIEF: Envy? Longing for power?

KHLUDOV: Oh, no, no. I hate you for dragging me into all of this. Where are the promised Allied forces? Where is the Russian Empire? How could you start the fight against them when you're powerless? Do you have any idea of the hate a man must feel when he knows that nothing will come of his actions, and yet must act? It is because of you that I am sick! (*Quieting down.*) However, this is not the time, we are both passing into nonbeing.

COMMANDER IN CHIEF: I advise you to remain here in the palace. This is the best way to make sure you will pass into nonbeing.

KHLUDOV: That's an idea. But I have not yet thought it through to the end.

COMMANDER IN CHIEF: I am not detaining you, General.

KHLUDOV: Driving out the faithful servant? "Him, who in ceaseless battle spilled blood like water for thee?"*

COMMANDER IN CHIEF (*bangs the chair on the floor*): Clown!

---

* A letter from the rebel Prince Kurbsky to Ivan the Terrible, from the poem "Vasily Shibanov" by Alexey K. Tolstoy.

KHLUDOV: Alexander of Macedon is a hero, but why break chairs?

COMMANDER IN CHIEF (*flies into blind rage at the words "Alexander of Macedon"*): If you dare . . . another word! . . . If you . . .

CONVOY SOLDIER (*appears as if from nowhere*): Your Excellency, the Cavalry School from Simferopol is here. Everything is ready!

COMMANDER IN CHIEF: It is? We're going! (*To* KHLUDOV.) We shall meet again! (*Exits.*)

KHLUDOV (*alone, sits down by the fireplace, his back to the door*): Empty. That's good. (*Suddenly rises nervously and opens the door, revealing a series of dark, abandoned rooms with chandeliers wrapped in dark muslin bags.*) Hey, is anyone there? No, no one. (*Sits down.*) Well, now, do I remain? No, this does not solve my problem. (*Turns around and speaks to someone.*) Will you go away, or won't you? Such nonsense! I can walk through you, just as I walked through the fog the other day. (*Walks, as though through something.*) There, I've crushed you. (*Sits down, silent.*)

The door opens cautiously, and GOLUBKOV *enters. He is hatless, but in his coat.*

GOLUBKOV: For God's sake, let me come in for a moment!

KHLUDOV (*without turning*): Certainly, certainly, come in.

GOLUBKOV: I know this is extreme presumption, but I was promised that I would be admitted to see you. But everyone is gone, and so I entered.

KHLUDOV (*without turning*): What do you want with me?

GOLUBKOV: I have ventured to come here, Your Excellency, to report the most dreadful crimes taking place at the counter-intelligence department. I've hastened to come here to complain about the beastly crime committed on General Khludov's order. (KHLUDOV *turns around. Recognizing* KHLUDOV, GOLUBKOV *backs away.*) A-ah . . .

KHLUDOV: That's interesting. But, if you'll pardon me, you are alive, aren't you? You were not hanged, I hope? What is your complaint? (*Silence.*) You make a pleasant impression. I've seen you somewhere. Well, what is your complaint? And don't be cowardly, please. You've come to speak, then speak!

GOLUBKOV: Very well. The day before yesterday you ordered the arrest of a woman . . .

KHLUDOV: I remember. Yes, I remember. I recall it. I recognized you. But permit me, to whom did you intend to complain against me?

GOLUBKOV: The Commander in Chief.

KHLUDOV: You're late. He's gone. (*Points at the window.*)

Lights glimmer far away. The sky glows with distant fires.

A pail of water. He is sunk into nonbeing forever. There is no one any more to whom you could complain against General Khludov. (*He walks to the desk, picks up one of the telephones, and speaks into it.*) Anteroom? Captain Golovan . . . Take an escort, Captain, and go to the counter-intelligence building. There was a woman I arrested . . . (*To* GOLUBKOV.) Korzukhina?

GOLUBKOV: Yes, yes, Serafima Vladimirovna!

KHLUDOV (*into the telephone*): Serafima Vladimirovna Korzukhina. If she wasn't shot, bring her here to the palace at once. (*Puts down the receiver.*) We'll wait.

GOLUBKOV: If she wasn't shot, you said? If she wasn't shot? . . . Shot? Oh, if you did that . . . (*Weeps.*)

KHLUDOV: Be a man.

GOLUBKOV: Ah, so you mock me too! Very well, I will . . . If she is dead, I'll kill you!

KHLUDOV (*apathetically*): Well, that might be the best solution. But no, you won't kill anyone, unfortunately. Keep quiet. (GOLUBKOV *sits down in silence.* KHLUDOV *turns away from him and speaks to someone.*) Since you've become my companion, soldier, speak to me. Your silence oppresses me, although it seems to me that your voice must be heavy and brassy. Or else leave me. You know that I am a man of great will power. I will not give in to the first apparition, people get cured of that. You must realize that you've simply been caught in the wheel, and it destroyed you and crushed your bones. And there's no sense in tagging after me. Do you hear, my relentless eloquent orderly?

GOLUBKOV: To whom are you speaking?

KHLUDOV: What? To whom? We'll find out right away. (*He slices the air with his hand.*) To no one, to myself. Yes. And what is she to you, your mistress?

GOLUBKOV: No, no! I met her by chance, but I love her. Oh, what a wretched madman I am! Why did I get her up that night at the monastery when she was ill, why did I persuade her to come here, straight into the devil's paws! . . . Oh, what a miserable wretch I am!

KHLUDOV: Indeed, why did you come my way? What brought you here? And now, when the machine broke down, you come here to demand what I cannot give you. There is no Serafima, and there won't be. She was shot.

GOLUBKOV: Beast! Murderer! Senseless murderer!

KHLUDOV: Now I have them from two sides: the living, the absurd, the speaking one—and the silent orderly. What's happening to me? My soul is split, and I hear

words dimly, as through water into which I sink like
lead. Damn the two, they hang on my feet and pull
me down into the dark, and the dark calls me.

GOLUBKOV: Ah, now I see it! You are a madman! Now I
understand it all! The ice on the Chongar, and the
black bags, and the frost! Cruel fate! Why do you
mock me? Why did I fail to guard my Serafima? Here
he is, here he is, her blind murderer! And what can
be asked of him if his reason is gone?

KHLUDOV: What a fool! (*Throws a revolver to* GOLUBKOV.)
Do me a favor, fire. (*Into space.*) All right, leave me
alone. Perhaps this one will have sense enough to fire.

GOLUBKOV: No, I cannot fire at you! You're pitiful, you're
terrifying, you're revolting!

KHLUDOV: What sort of comedy is this?

The sound of steps in the distance.

Wait, wait, they're coming! Perhaps it's he? We'll
find out everything in a moment.

GOLOVAN *enters.*

Was she shot?

GOLOVAN: No, Sir.

GOLUBKOV: She is alive? She is alive? Where is she, where?

KHLUDOV: Quiet. (*To* GOLOVAN.) Then why haven't you
brought her here? (GOLOVAN *gives* GOLUBKOV *a sidelong
glance.*) You can speak before him.

GOLOVAN: Yes, Sir. At four o'clock this afternoon Major
General Charnota burst into the counter-intelligence
headquarters, and took her away, by threat of armed
force.

GOLUBKOV: Where to? Where?

KHLUDOV: Be quiet. (*To* GOLOVAN.)˙ Where?

GOLOVAN: Aboard the Viking. At five the Viking left the harbor, and after five it put out to the open sea.

KHLUDOV: That's all. Thank you. And so, you see, she is alive. Your woman, your Serafima, is alive.

GOLUBKOV: Yes, yes, alive, alive . . .

KHLUDOV: Captain, take the convoy and the flag and go on board the Saint, I'll be there soon.

GOLOVAN: Permit me to report . . .

KHLUDOV: I'm in my right mind, I'll come, don't be afraid, I'll come.

GOLOVAN: Yes, Sir. (*Disappears.*)

KHLUDOV: Well, so she is on the way—to Constantinople.

GOLUBKOV (*blindly*): Yes, yes, yes, to Constantinople . . . I will not leave her now, I'll follow her. Those lights, those lights in the port, look at them. You must take me with you to Constantinople.

KHLUDOV: Oh, damn it, damn it, damn it . . .

GOLUBKOV: Come, Khludov, hurry!

KHLUDOV: Be silent! (*Mutters.*) Well, I have satisfied one, now I can have a talk with you in peace. (*Into space.*) What do you want? You want me to remain? He doesn't answer. He grows dim, he moves away, he wrapped himself in darkness and stands there.

GOLUBKOV (*with anguish*): Khludov, you are sick! Khludov, this is a delusion! Leave him! We must hurry! The Saint will sail, we shall be late!

KHLUDOV: The devil . . . the devil . . . There's some woman, Serafima . . . To Constantinople . . . All right, we're going, we're going! (*Leaves rapidly.*)

GOLUBKOV *walks out after him.*

Darkness.

FIFTH DREAM

A *strange symphony. Turkish melodies and, intermingled with them, the strains of "The Parting," a Russian senti-mental song played on a hurdy-gurdy, the cries of street vendors, the rumble of moving streetcars.*

And suddenly Constantinople appears, lit up by the eve-ning sun. The rooftops are dominated by a minaret. A curi-ous structure, like a carousel, topped by a large sign in French, English, and Russian:
> STOP! THE SENSATION OF CONSTANTINOPLE!
> COCKROACH RACES!!!
> GAMBLING À LA RUSSE, WITH POLICE PERMISSION
> SENSATION À CONSTANTINOPLE! COURSES DES CAFARDS!
> ТАРАКАНЬИ БЕЛА!

The structure is decorated with flags of various nations. Box-office window, with signs SINGLES *and* DOUBLES. *Sign over box office in French and Russian,* BEGINNING AT 5 P.M., COMMENCEMENT À 5 HEURES DU SOIR. *At the side is an open-air restaurant with sickly laurels in tubs. Sign:* RUS-SIAN DELICACY—VOBLA. PORTION 50 PIASTERS. *Above it— made of painted plywood—a cockroach in a dress coat, serving a foaming mug of beer, with a laconic sign,* BEER.

Above and beyond the structure, the narrow lane lives its own life in the numbing heat. A succession of people: Turkish women in yashmaks, Turks in red fezes, foreign sailors in white; an occasional donkey loaded with baskets. A stall selling coconuts. Now and then a Russian in a shabby uniform is seen in the crowd. Tinkling bells of lemonade vendors. Somewhere an urchin howls desperately, "Presse du soir!"

CHARNOTA *comes out of the alley and walks toward the structure. He is wearing a Circassian coat without shoulder straps. He is gloomy, and has obviously had a few drinks despite the heat. He carries a tray on his stomach, loaded with rubber devils, mother-in-law's tongues, and little jumping dolls.*

CHARNOTA: It doesn't break, it doesn't crush, it jumps and tumbles! Buy a Red Commissar for the amusement of your little angels! Madame! Madame! Achetez pour vos enfants! Buy for your children!

TURKISH WOMAN (*a loving mother*): Bounun fia ty nadyr? Combien?

CHARNOTA: Cinquante piastres, madame, cinquante! Fifty piastres!

TURKISH WOMAN: O, yokh! Bu pakhaly dyr? Too much!

CHARNOTA: Madame! Forty! Quarante! A plague on you! You've never had any children anyway! Gehen sie! ... Gehen sie! ... Go to your harem! God, what a bitch of a city!

Constantinople moans above CHARNOTA. *Tenors are screaming somewhere; lemon vendors cry sweetly,*

"Ambulasi, Ambulasi!" Basses add to the symphony,
"Kaimaki, Kaimaki!" The molten heat flows over
everything. A woman's face appears in the box office.
CHARNOTA *walks over to it.*

Marya Konstantinovna, Marya Konstantinovna!
FACE: What can I do for you, Grigory Lukyanovich?
CHARNOTA: Well, you see . . . It's this . . . Can I possibly
place a bet on Janissary today—on credit?
FACE: Oh, Grigory Lukyanovich, how can you? How can I?
CHARNOTA: What do you think I am, a Constantinople
crook, or a freemason, or somebody you don't know?
I'd think you can trust a general who has his own
business next to the races!
FACE: Well, of course, you're right . . . But talk to Artur
Arturovich yourself.
CHARNOTA: Artur Arturovich!

ARTUR *appears above the carousel like Punch from*
behind a screen, struggling to button on his dress-shirt
collar.

ARTUR: What is it? Who needs me? Ah! . . . What can I
do for you?
CHARNOTA: Well, you see, I wanted to ask you . . .
ARTUR: No! (*Disappears.*)
CHARNOTA: The boor! Where did you go? I haven't finished.
ARTUR (*appears*): But I know what you're going to say.
CHARNOTA: That's interesting—and what is it?
ARTUR: Much less interesting than what I'll say to you.
CHARNOTA: That's interesting—and what is that?
ARTUR: No credit for anyone! (*Disappears.*)
CHARNOTA: The pig!

Two French sailors appear in the restaurant, shouting,

"Un bock! Un bock!" The waiter serves them beer.

FACE: A bedbug's crawling on you, Grigory Lukyanovich! Take it off.

CHARNOTA: To hell with it, I wouldn't trouble, it's useless. Let it crawl, it doesn't bother me. Eh, what a city! All the cities I've seen in my lifetime, but nothing like this . . . Oh, yes, I've seen many cities, enchanting cities, great ones!

FACE: What cities did you see, Grigory Lukyanovich?

CHARNOTA: Good Lord! What about Kharkov! And Rostov! And Kiev! Kiev—what a beauty that is, Marya Konstantinovna! The monastery all aflame in the hills, and the Dnieper, the Dnieper! Indescribable air, indescribable light! Grass, the smell of hay, the hillsides, the valleys, the ravines by the Dnieper! And the fine battle we had outside of Kiev, I remember it now, a glorious battle! It was warm, the sun was shining, warm but not hot, Marya Konstantinovna. And the lice, of course . . . A louse—there's an insect for you!

FACE: Phooey, what disgusting things you're saying, Grigory Lukyanovich!

CHARNOTA: Why disgusting? After all, you must understand, there are insects and insects. A louse is a military animal, it belongs on the battlefield. But a bedbug? A parasite. The louse travels in squadrons, in cavalry formation, it flows like lava, and then you know —there will be battles on the largest scale! (*Cries with anguish.*) Artur!

ARTUR (*in evening coat, looks out*): What are you yelling about?

CHARNOTA: I look at you, and I admire you, Artur! Now you're in evening dress. You're not a man, you are a marvel of creation—a cockroach king. Such luck! But then, your nation always has all the luck!

ARTUR: If you start again with your anti-Semitism, I won't speak to you.

CHARNOTA: What do you care? You said yourself you're a Hungarian.

ARTUR: All the same . . .

CHARNOTA: So that's what I'm saying—you Hungarians have all the luck! Look here, now, Artur Arturovich —I want to liquidate my enterprise. (*Points to his tray.*)

ARTUR: Fifty.

CHARNOTA: What?

ARTUR: Piastres.

CHARNOTA: Are you playing jokes with me? I sell them at fifty apiece!

ARTUR: Go on, then!

CHARNOTA: Do you intend to be a bloodsucker all your life?

ARTUR: I'm not forcing you.

CHARNOTA: You're fortunate, Artur Arturovich, you didn't come my way in Northern Tauria!

ARTUR: Thank God, this isn't Northern Tauria!

CHARNOTA: Take the cartridge belts too. They're silver.

ARTUR: The cartridge belts and the tray—two lire fifty.

CHARNOTA: Here, take them! (*Gives* ARTUR *the tray and the cartridge belts.*)

ARTUR: Here. (*Gives* CHARNOTA *the money.*)

Three men walk into the carousel. They are wearing hats with peacock feathers and sleeveless vests, and carry accordions. ARTUR *disappears, then looks out again and shouts.*

Five o'clock! We're starting! Come in, gentlemen!

*A tricolored Russian flag is raised over the carousel.
The accordions break into a gay march.* CHARNOTA *is
first at the box office.*

CHARNOTA: Come on, Marya Konstantinovna, two lire fifty
on Janissary!

*A crowd of people gathers at the box office. A group
of* ITALIAN SAILORS *bursts in, followed by* BRITISH SAIL-
ORS *and with them a* BEAUTIFUL PROSTITUTE. *Crooks
and swindlers of every kind. A Negro. The march
thunders gaily. The waiter rushes about in the restaurant, serving beer.* ARTUR, *in a top hat and evening
coat, rises above the carousel. The march is silenced.*

ARTUR: Ladies and gentlemen! The race is starting! Ex-
clusive game of the Russian Royal Court! Cockroach
races! Courses des cafards! Corso del piatello! Tara-
kanyi bega! Favorite amusement of the late Empress
at Tsarskoye Selo! L'amusement préféré de la défunte
impératrice Russe à Tsarskoye Selo!

Two policemen, Italian and Turkish, appear.

First event! Contestants: Number 1—Black Pearl!
Number 2—the favorite, Janissary.

ITALIAN SAILORS (*applaud, shout*): Evviva!

BRITISH SAILORS (*whistle, shout*): Away! Away!

A perspiring, excited FIGURE *in a derby, with shoulder
straps of the quartermaster corps, bursts in.*

FIGURE: Am I late? Are they running?

Voice: "You'll make it!"

ARTUR: Number 3—Baba Yaga! Number 4—Don't Cry,
Child! A dapple-gray cockroach!

Shouts: "Hurrah! Don't Cry, Child!" "It's a swindle!"
"It's a swindle!"

Number 6—Hooligan! Number 7—Button!

Whistles. Shouts: "A trap!" "A trap!"

I beg your pardon! Not a chance! The cockroaches
are running on an open board, with paper jockeys!
The cockroaches live in a sealed box under the care of
the professor of entomology of the Kazan Imperial
University, who barely managed to escape from the
hands of the Bolsheviks! And now, the start! (*Drops
down into the carousel.*)

*The crowd surges into the carousel. Urchins appear
atop the stone fence. Hum of voices in the carousel,
then dead silence. Then the accordions break out into
"The Moon is Shining." The rustle of running cockroach feet is heard through the music. A frantic voice
in the carousel: "They're off!" A Greek urchin, looking like an imp, dances on the fence, shouting: "Off,
off!" Cries in the carousel: "Janissary's out! He's out!
The race is fixed." Noise.*

CHARNOTA (*at the box office*): Out? It can't be!!!

*Voice in the carousel: "Don't Cry, Child!" Another
voice: "Come on, come on!"*

Your Artur! Killing him is not enough!

The FACE *anxiously looks out of the box office. The
policemen are nervous, look inside the carousel.*

FIGURE (*running out of the carousel*): A swindle! Artur got
Janissary drunk on beer!

ARTUR *breaks out of the carousel. The tails of his eve-*

*ning coat are torn off, his top hat is squashed into a
pancake, he has no collar. His face is bloody. A mob
of gamblers chases him.*

ARTUR (*yells desperately*): Marya Konstantinovna, call the
police!

The FACE *disappears. The policemen whistle.*

ITALIAN SAILORS (*shout*): Ladro! Scroccone! Trufatore!

BEAUTIFUL PROSTITUTE: Let him have it, Gianni! (*To*
ARTUR.) Ingannatore!

BRITISH SAILORS: Hip, hip, hurrah! Long live Button!

BEAUTIFUL PROSTITUTE: Brothers! Fratelli! Somebody
bribed Artur to play Button! The favorite just stands
there waving his feet, drunk as a fiddler! Who's ever
seen Janissary go wrong?

ARTUR (*in despair*): Where did you ever see a drunk cockroach? Je vous demande un peu, où est-ce que vous
avez vu un cafard soûl? Police! Police! Au secours!
Police! Help!

BEAUTIFUL PROSTITUTE: Mensonge! He's lying! Everybody
bet on Janissary! Get him, the swindler!

ITALIAN SAILOR (*seizes* ARTUR *by the throat, shouts*): Ah,
marmalia!

ITALIAN SAILORS (*shout*): Canalia!

ARTUR (*soulfully*): They're killing me . . .

BRITISH SAILOR (*to the* ITALIAN SAILOR): Stop! Keep back!
(*Seizes him.*)

FIGURE: Punch him on the ear!

BEAUTIFUL PROSTITUTE (*to the* BRITISH SAILOR): Ah, you'll
defend him?!

The BRITISH SAILOR *hits the* ITALIAN, *who falls.*

A soccoroso, fratelli! Help him, brothers! Give it to the English! Italians, help!

The British and the Italians fight. The Italians pull out their knives. At the sight of the knives, the crowd howls and scatters in all directions. The Greek urchin dances on the wall and shouts, "They're butchering the English!" A mob of Italian and Turkish police armed with revolvers bursts in, whistling, from the alley. CHARNOTA, *at the box office, clutches his head.*

Sudden dissolve. Darkness. Silence.

*. . . Parting, cruel parting! . . .**

SIXTH DREAM

Out of the darkness appears a courtyard with cypresses, a two-story house with a terrace. Water tank by the stone wall; quiet tapping of water drops. Stone bench near the gate. Beyond the house, a twisting deserted alley. The sun is setting behind the balustrade of a minaret. First evening shadows. Quiet.

CHARNOTA (*enters the courtyard*): Damned Button! However, that is not the point, the point is that I am done for, finished . . . She'll eat me alive, she will. Clear out? But where to, if I may ask you, Grigory Lukyanovich, where can I go? This isn't Tauria, you're not supposed to run from here. Oh, oh!

The door to the terrace opens and LYUSKA *comes out. She is carelessly dressed. She is hungry, and this makes her eyes glitter and lends her face a fleeting, unearthly beauty.*

LYUSKA: Ah, a good day to you, Your Excellency! Bonjour, Madame Barabanchikova!

---

* From a Russian popular song.

CHARNOTA: Hello, Lyusenka!

LYUSKA: But why so early? If I were in your place, I'd hang around in town till all hours, especially since it's no fun at home—no food, no money. But I see happy news on your expressive face, and the tray is gone. And the cartridge belts are absent. I think I am beginning to understand. The money, if you please! Serafima and I had nothing to eat since yesterday. Kindly!

CHARNOTA: Where is Serafima?

LYUSKA: That's unimportant. She's doing the laundry. Come on, let's have the money.

CHARNOTA: There's been a catastrophe, Lyusenka.

LYUSKA: Really? And where are the cartridge belts?

CHARNOTA: Well, you see, Lyusenka, I thought I'd sell them, so I put them into the tray, then I took off the tray for a moment at the Grand Bazaar, and . . .

LYUSKA: Stolen?

CHARNOTA: U-huh . . .

LYUSKA: Of course, it was a man with a black beard, wasn't it?

CHARNOTA (*weakening*): What has a man with a black beard to do with it?

LYUSKA: Oh, he always steals from sons of bitches at the Grand Bazaar. So they were stolen? Your word of honor? (CHARNOTA *nods.*) In that case, I'll tell you something. Do you know, Grisha, what you are?

CHARNOTA: What?

LYUSKA: A filthy bastard!

CHARNOTA: How dare you?

SERAFIMA *comes out with a pail, stops. They don't notice her.*

LYUSKA: I dare, because the tray was bought with my money!

CHARNOTA: You're my wife, and our money belongs to both.

LYUSKA: The husband earns his money by selling imps, and the wife, by selling something altogether different!

CHARNOTA: What did you say?

LYUSKA: Stop playing the fool! Do you think I went out with that Frenchman last week to sing hymns? Did anybody ask me where I got those five lire? No, but we all lived on them for a week—you, and I, and Serafima! But that isn't all! The tray and the cartridge belts were not lost at the Grand Bazaar, they were lost at the cockroach races! All right, let's sum it up. The bold knight General Charnota wrecked the counter-intelligence headquarters and had to flee from the army, and now he's starving in Constantinople, and I'm starving with him!

CHARNOTA: Are you reproaching me for saving a woman from death? Are you reproaching me for Simka?

LYUSKA: No! But I can reproach Simka! (*Loses all restraint.*) Let the immaculate Serafima go on sighing for her lost Golubkov, let her go on living in peace, let the brilliant general go on living in peace at the expense of the slut Lyuska!

SERAFIMA: Lyusya!

LYUSKA: Eavesdropping doesn't seem to become you, Serafima Vladimirovna!

SERAFIMA: I never dreamed of eavesdropping. I heard you accidentally, and I'm glad I did. Why didn't you say anything about the five lire before?

LYUSKA: Stop pretending, Serafima, are you blind, or what?

SERAFIMA: I swear to you I didn't know. I thought he brought the money. But don't worry, Lyusya, I'll make it up.

LYUSKA: No noble gestures, please!

SERAFIMA: Don't be angry, let's not quarrel. Let us take a look at the situation.

LYUSKA: There's nothing to look at. Tomorrow the Greeks will kick us out of this place, we have nothing to eat, everything is sold. (*Flies into a rage again.*) No, I can't calm down! He burns me up! (*To* CHARNOTA.) Answer me, you gambled it away?

CHARNOTA: I did.

LYUSKA: Oh, you! . . .

CHARNOTA: But try to see my position! I cannot peddle imps! I was a soldier!

SERAFIMA: Forget it, Lyusya, forget it . . . Please, forget it! Two or three lire, what difference would they make? (*Silence.*) But really, an evil fate seems to pursue us!

LYUSKA: Poetry!

CHARNOTA (*suddenly, to* LYUSKA): You went with the Frenchman?

LYUSKA: Aw, go to hell, leave me alone!

SERAFIMA: Be quiet, be quiet! Stop fighting, I'll bring supper in a moment.

LYUSKA: Quit, Simka, it's not for you. Don't be offended at my words. I'll take this road anyway. I won't go hungry, I have no principles!

SERAFIMA: I won't go hungry, either, and I won't live at someone else's expense. To sit here, knowing that you go into the street to make some money? . . . I couldn't be that low! You should have told me. We're in a hole together, and together we'll do what we can!

LYUSKA: Charnota will sell the revolver.

CHARNOTA: Lyusenka, I'll sell my pants, I'll sell anything, but not the revolver! I cannot live without the revolver!

LYUSKA: He's got a revolver instead of a head. All right, then, live off women!

CHARNOTA: Don't provoke me!

LYUSKA: Just touch me with one finger, I'll poison you at night!

SERAFIMA: Stop it! Squabbling all the time! I tell you, we'll have supper! It's only because you're hungry!

LYUSKA: What do you have in mind, you fool?

SERAFIMA: I'm not a fool, but I was a fool! What's the difference what you sell? It's all such nonsense! (*Goes back to the terrace, and returns with her hat on. Speaks as she is leaving.*) Wait for me, but please, no fighting.

A hurdy-gurdy is heard somewhere, playing "The Parting."

LYUSKA: Simka! Simka!

CHARNOTA: Sima!

Silence.

LYUSKA: Ugh, what a vile city! Ugh, the bedbugs! Ugh, the Bosphorus! . . . And you . . .

CHARNOTA: Be quiet.

LYUSKA: I hate you, and I hate myself, and I hate all Russians! Damned have-beens! (*Exits to the terrace.*)

CHARNOTA (*alone*): Where now? Paris, Berlin? Or perhaps Madrid? A Spanish city . . . Never saw it. But I bet it's a hole. (*Squats down, feels for something with his hand under the cypress, finds a cigarette butt.*) Tight people, those Greeks, smoke to the very end, the sons of bitches! No, I don't agree with her, our Russians are better, definitely better. (*Lights the butt and exits to the terrace.*)

GOLUBKOV *enters the courtyard. He is wearing an Eng-*

lish jacket, leg wrappings, and a Turkish fez. He carries a hurdy-gurdy, which he puts down on the ground and begins to play "The Parting," then a march. CHARNOTA *shouts from the terrace.*

Stop tearing my guts out, you Turkish monkey!

GOLUBKOV: What? Gri . . . Grigory Lukyanovich? I said I'd find you! I found you!

CHARNOTA: Who's that? You, Professor?

GOLUBKOV (*overcome with emotion, sits down on the edge of the water tank*): I found you.

CHARNOTA (*comes running down*): You found me all right, you did . . . And I thought you were a Turk. Hello, hello! (*Kisses him.*) But what you look like! Eh, you've aged! We thought you remained with the Bolsheviks. Where have you been these six months?

GOLUBKOV: First in the camp, then I caught typhus, two months in the hospital, and now I'm tramping all over Constantinople. Khludov took me in. They threw him out, they threw him out of the army, you know.

CHARNOTA: I heard. I'm a civilian myself now. We've been through everything here . . . But you're the first one with a hurdy-gurdy.

GOLUBKOV: It's just the thing for me, the hurdy-gurdy. I go from yard to yard, searching. But tell me straight out, is she dead? Don't be afraid, tell me. I'm used to everything now.

CHARNOTA: Ah, Serafima? No, why dead? She has recovered, she's alive and well!

GOLUBKOV: I found her! (*Embraces* CHARNOTA.)

CHARNOTA: Sure, she is alive. But I must say, we're in a bad hole, Professor! Everything's smashed. We are at the end of the rope, Seryozha!

GOLUBKOV: But where is she, where is Serafima?

CHARNOTA: She's here. She'll be here soon. She went out to look for a man on the Pera.

GOLUBKOV: What?

CHARNOTA: Don't stare at me! We're croaking with hunger. No cartridge belts, no money.

GOLUBKOV: What do you mean—she went to the Pera? You're lying!

CHARNOTA: Huh, lying! And me, I haven't had a smoke all day. There's something that keeps drawing me to Madrid . . . I dreamed of Madrid all night . . .

Voices. SERAFIMA *enters, followed by a* GREEK DON JUAN, *loaded with purchases and bottles.*

SERAFIMA: Oh, no, no, it will be fine, we'll sit and chat a while . . . Of course, we live like gypsies here . . .

GREEK DON JUAN (*with a strong accent*): Very, very charming! I am afraid of inconveniencing you, Madame.

SERAFIMA: Let me introduce you . . . (CHARNOTA *turns his back on her.*) Grigory Lukyanovich, where are you going, you embarrass me!

GREEK DON JUAN: Very, very pleased!

SERAFIMA (*recognizes* GOLUBKOV): Oh, God!

GOLUBKOV, *frowning painfully, gets up from the tank, walks over to the Greek and punches him on the ear. The* GREEK DON JUAN *drops his parcels, looks sad. Anxious Greek and Armenian heads appear in the windows.* LYUSKA *comes out on the terrace.*

GREEK DON JUAN: What is this? This is what?

SERAFIMA: Oh, God! . . . The shame, the shame!

CHARNOTA: Monsieur Greek!

GREEK DON JUAN: Ah, I am captured in a flytrap, a den! (*He is very sad.*)

SERAFIMA: Forgive me, Monsieur, forgive me, for God's sake! This is terrible, it's a misunderstanding!

CHARNOTA (*takes his revolver and turns to the windows*): Beat it, this minute! (*The heads vanish and the windows close.*)

GREEK DON JUAN (*mournfully*): Oh, my God . . .

GOLUBKOV (*advances upon him*): You . . .

GREEK DON JUAN (*takes out his wallet and his watch*): Take my wallet, take my watch, brave man! My life is dear—I have a family, a store, little children . . . I'll never say a word to the police . . . Live, my good man, and praise the Lord Almighty . . .

GOLUBKOV: Get out!

GREEK DON JUAN: Ah, Stamboul, what has become of you! . . .

GOLUBKOV: Get your parcels!

The GREEK DON JUAN *wants to pick up his parcels, but takes a look at Golubkov's face, turns and runs.*

LYUSKA: Golubkov? And we were talking about you just an hour ago! We thought you were in Russia. But I must say, you made a brilliant entrance!

GOLUBKOV: And you, Serafima Vladimirovna, what are you doing? I sailed and I ran, I was in the hospital—you can see my head is shaved . . . I thought only of finding you! And you, what are you doing?

SERAFIMA: Who gave you the right to reproach me?

GOLUBKOV: I love you, I followed you to tell you!

SERAFIMA: Leave me alone. I don't want to hear any more! I'm sick of everything! Why did you come again? We're all beggars! I cut myself off from all of you! . . . I want to perish alone! God, what a shame! What a disgrace! Goodbye!

GOLUBKOV: Don't go, I beg you!

SERAFIMA: I'll never come back! (*Leaves.*)

GOLUBKOV: So that's how it is! (*Snatches Charnota's dagger and rushes after* SERAFIMA.)

CHARNOTA (*throws his arms around him and takes away the dagger*): Have you gone mad? You want a taste of prison?

GOLUBKOV: Let me go! I'll find her anyway, I'll stop her! Oh, hell! (*Sits down again on the edge of the tank.*)

LYUSKA: What a show, what a show! The Greeks are stunned. All right, that will do. Charnota, open the parcels, I'm hungry.

GOLUBKOV: I won't let you touch the parcels!

CHARNOTA: I won't open them.

LYUSKA: Ah, I see! Well, my patience is gone! I've drunk my cup to the bottom. That's it! (*Gets her hat and a package, and comes down.*) Well, Grigory Lukyanovich, the best of luck to you. Our life together is finished. Lyuska knows people on the Orient Express, and Lyuska was a fool to stick around here for half a year! Goodbye!

CHARNOTA: Where are you going?

LYUSKA: To Paris! To Paris! Goodbye! (*Disappears in the alley.*)

CHARNOTA *and* GOLUBKOV *sit on the edge of the water tank. Both are silent. A Turkish urchin is guiding someone, beckoning to him, saying, "Here, here!" The boy is followed by* KHLUDOV, *in civilian clothes. He has aged and turned gray.*

CHARNOTA: And there's Roman. He's here too. What are you staring at—the cartridge belts are gone? I'm like you, a free man.

KHLUDOV: Yes, I see. Well, hello to you, Grigory Lukyanovich. We all seem to follow in each other's tracks. (*Points at* GOLUBKOV.) First I tried to cure him, and now he's dreaming of curing me. And in between, he plays the hurdy-gurdy. (*To* GOLUBKOV.) Well, still no results?

GOLUBKOV: No, I found her. But don't ask me any questions. Don't ask me any questions.

KHLUDOV: I'm not asking. It's your affair. I only want to know if you found her.

GOLUBKOV: Khludov! I beg you, just one thing, you're the only one who can do it. Catch up with her, she left me, stop her, take care of her, don't let her go into the streets.

KHLUDOV: But why can't you do it yourself?

GOLUBKOV: As I was sitting here on the tank, I made a firm resolution, I'm going to Paris. I'll find Korzukhin. He is a rich man, he must help her, he ruined her.

KHLUDOV: How will you go? Who'll let you into France?

GOLUBKOV: I'll get through. I was playing the hurdy-gurdy in port today, there was a captain who was sympathetic. He said he'd stow me away in the hold and take me to Marseilles.

KHLUDOV: Oh, well. And how long will I have to watch over her?

GOLUBKOV: I'll be back soon, and I swear to you I'll never ask you for anything again.

KHLUDOV: I've been paying a heavy price for that station. (*Turning around.*) No, not here.

CHARNOTA (*in a whisper*): A fine guardian!

GOLUBKOV (*in a whisper*): Don't look at him, he is fighting it.

KHLUDOV: Where did she go?

CHARNOTA: That isn't hard to guess. She went to beg the Greek's forgiveness, he's at the commission store on Shishly Street. I know him.

KHLUDOV: All right, then.

GOLUBKOV: But see she does not go into the streets!

KHLUDOV: With me? Not with me watching her. Didn't a certain orderly say to me—nobody can get past you? . . . However, let's not return to that . . . "O Lord God, remember me!"* (To GOLUBKOV.) You have no money?

GOLUBKOV: I don't need any money!

KHLUDOV: Don't be a fool. Here's two lire, I haven't any more now. (*Detaches the medallion from his watch.*) Take the medallion. If worst comes to worst, you can sell it. (*Exits.*)

The evening shadows grow more dense. The sweet voice of the muezzin flows from the minaret, "La ilāha illa allāh . . ."†

GOLUBKOV: Night is coming! A deadful city! An intolerable city! A stifling city! But why am I sitting here? It's time! At night I shall sail in the hold.

CHARNOTA: I'm coming with you. We won't get any money. I have no hope of that, but anyway, a man must go somewhere. As I said, I was thinking of Madrid, but in fact, Paris is somehow even more appropriate. Let's go. The Greeks, our landlords, will have a pleasant surprise!

GOLUBKOV: It's never cool, not in the daytime, not at night!

CHARNOTA (*exits with him*): So now it's Paris!

---

* Judg. 16:28
† There is no God but Allah.

The Turkish urchin runs over to the hurdy-gurdy and turns the handle. It plays a march. The muezzin's voice is singing in the minaret. Shadows. Lights going on here and there. A pale golden horn in the sky. Then darkness.

Act Four

*"Three cards, three cards, three cards ..."**

SEVENTH DREAM

Autumn in Paris. Sunset. Monsieur Korzukhin's study in his own house. The study is furnished very impressively. Among other things, there is a fireproof safe. In addition to a desk, there is a card table. Two unlit candles stand on it, and a deck of cards lies ready.

KORZUKHIN: Antoine!

His valet, ANTOINE, *enters. He looks French and dignified, and wears a green apron.*

Monsieur Marchand m'avait averti qu'il ne viendra pas aujourd'hui. Ne remuez pas la table. Je me servirai plus tard. (*Silence.*) Repondez-donc quelque chose!† But it seems to me you didn't understand a single word?

ANTOINE: No, sir, Paramon Ilyich, I didn't.

KORZUKHIN: How do you say "no, sir" in French?

ANTOINE: I wouldn't know, Paramon Ilyich.

---

* From *The Queen of Spades*.

† Monsieur Marchand said he would not come today. Don't clear the table. I shall dine later. Answer me!

KORZUKHIN: Antoine, you're a lazy Russian good for nothing. A man who lives in Paris must realize that the Russian language is good only for obscenities or, even worse, for proclaiming destructive slogans. Neither one nor the other is the thing in Paris. You must try to learn, Antoine, it's a bore. Que faites-vous, en ce moment? What are you doing at this moment?

ANTOINE: Je . . . I'm polishing knives, Paramon Ilyich.

KORZUKHIN: How do you say "knives," Antoine?

ANTOINE: Le couteau, Paramon Ilyich.

KORZUKHIN: Right. Study, study, Antoine. (*The bell rings.* KORZUKHIN *unbuttons his pajama jacket as he walks toward the door.*) Answer the bell. Perhaps a partner will turn up. Je suis à la maison.* (*Exits.*)

ANTOINE *exits and returns with* GOLUBKOV, *dressed in black sailor's pants and a short gray threadbare coat, with a cap in his hands.*

GOLUBKOV: Je voudrais parler à Monsieur Korzukhin.†

ANTOINE: Your calling card, please, votre carte.

GOLUBKOV: Oh! You're Russian? And I took you for a Frenchman. I'm so glad!

ANTOINE: Yes, sir, I'm Russian. I'm Grishchenko.

GOLUBKOV *shakes hands with* ANTOINE.

GOLUBKOV: Well, you see, I have no card. Simply tell him it's Golubkov from Constantinople.

ANTOINE: Yes, sir. (*Exits.*)

KORZUKHIN (*comes out, wearing a jacket, mumbles*): What Golubkov? . . . Golubkov . . . What can I do for you?

---

* I am at home.

† I should like to speak to Mr. Korzukhin.

GOLUBKOV: You probably don't recognize me. We met a year ago, on that terrible night at the station in the Crimea, when your wife was arrested. She is now in Constantinople, she's on the verge of ruin.

KORZUKHIN: On the verge of what? Pardon me, in the first place, I have no wife, and in the second place, I don't recall any station.

GOLUBKOV: But of course! That night . . . and that frightful frost, do you remember the frost when the Crimea was taken?

KORZUKHIN: Sorry, I don't remember any frost. You are surely mistaken.

GOLUBKOV: But you are Paramon Ilyich Korzukhin, you were in the Crimea, I recognize you!

KORZUKHIN: It is true that I spent a short time in the Crimea, when those crazy generals were carrying on there. But, you see, I left very soon. I have no contacts with Russia and don't intend to have any. I have adopted French citizenship, I have never been married, and I must tell you that for the past two months a Russian émigré has been living in my house as my secretary. She has also adopted French citizenship and the name of Frejol. This most enchanting creature has touched my heart so deeply that, I will tell you in secret, I intend to marry her very soon. So that all this talk about some alleged wife of mine is extremely unpleasant to me.

GOLUBKOV: Frejol . . . So you repudiate a living human being! But she was coming to join you! You remember, she was arrested? Remember the frost, the windows, the street light like a blue moon?

KORZUKHIN: Yes, yes, a blue moon, frost . . . The counter-intelligence has already tried once to blackmail me with some sort of an imaginary Communist wife. I repeat to you, Monsieur Golubkov, I find this conversation unpleasant.

GOLUBKOV: Good God, I am dreaming my life! ...

KORZUKHIN: Undoubtedly.

GOLUBKOV: I see. She interferes with you. Very well. Let's say she is not your wife. It's even better that way. I love her, you understand? And I will do everything I can to save her from the clutches of poverty. But I appeal to you, help her at least for a short time. You are a very rich man, everybody knows that all your capital is abroad. Lend me a thousand dollars. As soon as we get to our feet, I'll return it, I swear. I'll earn it! I'll make it the goal of my existence.

KORZUKHIN: Forgive me, Monsieur Golubkov, that's precisely what I expected. I knew this talk of a mythical wife would lead to dollars. A thousand? Did I hear you right?

GOLUBKOV: A thousand. I swear, I will return it.

KORZUKHIN: Ah, my dear young man! Before you talk about a thousand dollars, I'll tell you what a single dollar means. (*Launches into a paean about the dollar, becoming more and more inspired.*) The dollar! That great omnipotent spirit! It is everywhere! Take a look there! There, far away, on a roof, a golden sunray burns, and next to it, high in the air, is a crouching black cat—a chimera! The dollar is there, too! The chimera is guarding it! (*Points mysteriously to the floor.*) A vague emanation, not a noise, not a sound, but, as it were, the very breath of the bulging earth: trains are flying there as swift as arrows, and they carry the dollar. Now shut your eyes and imagine—darkness, and waves as huge as mountains. Darkness and water— the ocean! It is terrifying, it will devour you. But a monster moves through the ocean, with hissing boilers,

churning up millions of tons of water. It moves, groan-
ing, carrying lights! It plows up the water, it strains, but
in the infernal boiler rooms the naked stokers tend
the flames, and in its belly it carries its golden child,
its divine heart—the dollar! And suddenly the world
is troubled! (*Sounds of military music in the distance.*)
And now they come! They come! They come in the
thousands, and then in the millions! Their heads are
encased in steel helmets. They walk! Then they run!
Then they throw themselves upon barbed wire! Why?
Because the sacred dollar was insulted somewhere! But
now the world is at peace, and trumpets blare triumphantly in every city! It is avenged! They blow in
honor of the dollar! (*Calms down. Music recedes.*)
And so, Monsieur Golubkov, I think that now you
will no longer insist on my handing an unknown young
man a thousand dollars.

GOLUBKOV: No, I will not insist. But I would like to say to
you in parting, Monsieur Korzukhin, that you are the
most soulless, the most terrible man I have ever met.
And you will get your punishment. It will come! It
must come! Goodbye! (*Turns to leave.*)

The bell rings. ANTOINE *enters.*

ANTOINE: General Charnota.

KORZUKHIN: Hm . . . A Russian day. Well, let him in, let
him in.

ANTOINE *leaves.* CHARNOTA *enters. He is wearing a
Circassian coat, but without the silver belt and without
the dagger. Under the coat he wears lemon-yellow
underpants. The expression on his face shows that he
has nothing to lose. He is free and easy in his manner.*

CHARNOTA: Hi, Paramosha!

KORZUKHIN: Have we ever met?

CHARNOTA: What a question! Are you asleep, Paramon? What about Sebastopol?

KORZUKHIN: Oh, yes, of course . . . Very pleased. Pardon me, but did we ever drink Brüderschaft?

CHARNOTA: Who the devil remembers . . . But if we met, we must have drunk.

KORZUKHIN: Excuse me, please, but you seem to be wearing underpants?

CHARNOTA: Why does it surprise you? I am not a woman, for whom this type of garment would be inappropriate.

KORZUKHIN: You . . . You walked through the Paris streets like that, General?

CHARNOTA: No, I walked in the street in trousers, but I took them off in your foyer. What an idiotic question!

KORZUKHIN: Sorry, sorry.

CHARNOTA (*quietly to* GOLUBKOV): Did you get it?

GOLUBKOV: No. I'm leaving. Let's get out of here.

CHARNOTA: And where can we go now? (*To* KORZUKHIN.) What's the matter with you, Paramon? Your countrymen, who fought against the Bolsheviks for you, come to you, and you refuse them a trifling sum. Do you understand that Serafima is starving in Constantinople?

GOLUBKOV: I'll beg you to keep quiet. In short, let's go, Grigory!

CHARNOTA: Well, you know, Paramon, sinful man that I am, I would deliberately join the Bolsheviks just to shoot you. I'd shoot you, and I'd quit the party that very moment. Wait, what are these cards for? Do you play?

KORZUKHIN: What's so strange about it? I do, and I'm very fond of it.

CHARNOTA: You play! And what's your game?

KORZUKHIN: Chemin de fer, and I'm very fond of it.

CHARNOTA: All right, let's have a game.

KORZUKHIN: I'd be delighted, but, you see, I like to play for cash only.

GOLUBKOV: Will you stop humiliating yourself, Grigory? Come on!

CHARNOTA: There's nothing humiliating about it. (*In a whisper.*) What did he tell you? If worst comes to worst? Well, this is it. Let me have Khludov's medallion!

GOLUBKOV: Here, you can have it, nothing matters to me any more. And I'm leaving.

CHARNOTA: Oh, no, we'll leave together. I won't let you go with that long face. Who knows, you may take a dive in the Seine. (*Holds out the medallion to* KORZUKHIN.) How much?

KORZUKHIN: Hm . . . Not bad . . . Oh, well, ten dollars.

CHARNOTA: After all, Paramon! This little article is worth much more, but you are evidently no judge of such things. Very well, it's sold! (*Gives* KORZUKHIN *the medallion and receives ten dollars from him. He sits down at the card table, rolls back the sleeves of his Circassian coat, shuffles the deck.*) What do you call your slave?

KORZUKHIN: Hm . . . Antoine.

CHARNOTA (*in a stentorian voice*): Antoine!

ANTOINE *appears.*

Bring me a bite of something, my good man.

ANTOINE (*with an astonished, but deferential smile*): Yes, sir . . . À l'instant! (*Disappears.*)

CHARNOTA: The stake?

KORZUKHIN: Oh, let's make it those ten dollars. Cards, please.

CHARNOTA: Nine.

KORZUKHIN (*pays*): Banco, if you please.

CHARNOTA (*deals*): Nine.

KORZUKHIN: Banco again.

CHARNOTA: Card?

KORZUKHIN: Yes. Seven.

CHARNOTA: I have eight.

KORZUKHIN (*with a smile*): Oh, well, Banco.

GOLUBKOV (*suddenly*): Charnota! What are you doing? He is doubling, he'll take everything back from you now!

CHARNOTA: If you understand the game better than I, take over for me.

GOLUBKOV: I don't know how.

CHARNOTA: Then keep out of my light! A card?

KORZUKHIN: Yes, please. Oh, damn, zero!

CHARNOTA: Three.

KORZUKHIN: You don't draw with three?

CHARNOTA: Sometimes, it depends . . .

ANTOINE *brings hors d'oeuvres.*

A drink, Golubkov?

GOLUBKOV: I don't want any.

CHARNOTA: And you, Paramon, why don't you help yourself?

KORZUKHIN: Merci, I've had my breakfast.

CHARNOTA: Aha . . . A card for you?

KORZUKHIN: Please. One hundred and sixty dollars.

CHARNOTA: On. "Countess, for a single rendezvous . . ." Nine.

KORZUKHIN: Never saw anything like it! Three hundred and twenty!

CHARNOTA: Cash, if you please.

GOLUBKOV: Stop, Charnota, I beg you! Stop now!

CHARNOTA: Do me a kindness, find yourself something to do. Look through an album, or something. (*To* KORZUKHIN.) Cash, please!

KORZUKHIN: One moment.

Opens the safe, which sets up a furious ringing throughout the apartment. The light goes out and flashes on again. ANTOINE *appears from the foyer with a gun in his hand.*

GOLUBKOV: What's this?

KORZUKHIN: Burglar alarm. It's all right, Antoine, it was I who opened it.

ANTOINE *exits.*

CHARNOTA: A nice gadget. Let's see now! Eight!

KORZUKHIN: Six hundred and forty dollars?

CHARNOTA: No bet. The bank will not accept the stake.

KORZUKHIN: You play well. How much will you accept?

CHARNOTA: Fifty.

KORZUKHIN: It's on! Nine!

CHARNOTA: Zero.

KORZUKHIN: Cash, please.

CHARNOTA: Certainly.

KORZUKHIN: Five hundred and ninety!

CHARNOTA: Eh, Paramosha, you're a gambler! That's your weak spot!

GOLUBKOV: Charnota, I beg you, come!

KORZUKHIN: Card! Seven!

CHARNOTA: Seven and a half! I'm joking, eight.

GOLUBKOV *suddenly moans, covers his ears, and stretches out on the sofa.* KORZUKHIN *opens the safe with a key. Again the ringing, the darkness, the light.*

*And now it is night on the stage. Candles are burning on
the card table, under little pink shades.* KORZUKHIN *is without his jacket, his hair is disheveled. The lights of Paris can
be seen through the window, music is heard somewhere.
Piles of money before* KORZUKHIN *and* CHARNOTA. GOLUBKOV
is sleeping on the sofa.

CHARNOTA (*sings under his breath*):"You will receive the
mortal stroke . . . three cards, three cards, three
cards . . ." Zero.

KORZUKHIN: Cash, please, four hundred! Three thousand?

CHARNOTA: It's on. Cash!

KORZUKHIN *rushes to the safe. Again the lights go out,
the ringing and music. Then light. Blue dawn in Paris.
Quiet. No music is heard.* KORZUKHIN, CHARNOTA *look
like shadows. Empty champagne bottles litter the floor.*
GOLUBKOV *crumples the money and stuffs it into his
pockets.* CHARNOTA *turns to* KORZUKHIN.

Do you have a newspaper to wrap it in?

KORZUKHIN: No. I'll tell you what, give me the cash, I'll
write you a check!

CHARNOTA: Really, Paramon! What bank will issue twenty
thousand dollars to a man in underpants? No, thanks!

GOLUBKOV: Charnota, buy back the medallion, I want to
return it.

KORZUKHIN: Three hundred dollars!

GOLUBKOV: There! (*Throws him the money. In return,*
KORZUKHIN *throws him the medallion.*)

CHARNOTA: Goodbye, Paramosha. We've stayed too long,
it's time to go.

KORZUKHIN (*barring the door*): No, wait! I have fever, I

don't understand anything . . . You took advantage of my sickness! Listen, give me back the money, I'll pay you off, five hundred dollars each!

CHARNOTA: " 'You're jesting,' cried the evil beast!"

KORZUKHIN: Well, if that's the case, I will phone the police right away, I'll say you robbed me! You'll be arrested at once! Tramps!

CHARNOTA: Did you hear? (*Takes out his revolver.*) Well, Paramon, pray to your Paris Notre Dame, your dying hour has come!

KORZUKHIN: Help! Help!

ANTOINE *comes running, in his underwear.*

Everybody is asleep! The whole villa is asleep! Nobody hears how I am being robbed! Help!

The draperies are pushed aside, and LYUSKA *appears. She is in pajamas. Seeing* CHARNOTA *and* GOLUBKOV, *she freezes.*

You're sleeping, dear Luci, while your patron is being robbed by Russian bandits!

LYUSKA: Oh, my God, my God! I guess I didn't drain my bitter cup to the very end yet! . . . I'd think I have a right to get some peace, but no, no . . . No wonder I dreamed of cockroaches tonight. I'd like to know one thing—how did you manage to get here?

CHARNOTA (*stunned*): It is she?

KORZUKHIN (*to* CHARNOTA): You know Mademoiselle Frejol?

LYUSKA *drops on her knees behind Korzukhin's back and pleadingly folds her hands.*

CHARNOTA: How would I know her? I've no idea.

LYUSKA: Then let us introduce ourselves, gentlemen! Luci Frejol.

CHARNOTA: General Charnota.

LYUSKA: Well, gentlemen, what's the trouble? (*To* KORZUKHIN.) My little rat, what were you squealing about so frantically, who hurt you?

KORZUKHIN: He won twenty thousand dollars from me! And I want him to return it!

GOLUBKOV: Who ever heard of such a thing!

LYUSKA: No, no, my little toad, that's impossible! If you lost it, you lost it! You're not a child!

KORZUKHIN: Where did Antoine buy those cards?

ANTOINE: You bought them yourself, Paramon Ilyich.

LYUSKA: Antoine, go to the devil! Hanging around in that state before me! (*He disappears.*) Gentlemen! The money belongs to you, and there will be no trouble. (*To* KORZUKHIN.) Go, my boy, go to sleep, go to sleep. You have shadows under your eyes.

KORZUKHIN: I'll fire that idiot Antoine! No Russian will ever set foot in my house again! (*Walks out with a sob.*)

LYUSKA: Well, now, I was delighted to see my countrymen and regret that we shall never meet again. (*Whispers.*) You won it, clear out! (*Loudly.*) Antoine!

ANTOINE *peeks in the door.*

The gentlemen are leaving, see them out.

CHARNOTA: Au revoir, Mademoiselle.

LYUSKA: Adieu.

CHARNOTA *and* GOLUBKOV *leave.*

Thank God, they're gone! Heavens! When will I ever have some peace? (*Steps are heard in the deserted street. Glancing around stealthily, she runs to the window, opens it and calls out quietly.*) Goodbye! Golubkov, take care of Serafima! Charnota! Buy yourself a pair of trousers!

Darkness.

EIGHTH DREAM

A room with rugs everywhere. Low divans. A narghile. A solid glass wall in the background, with a glass door. Behind the glass, the Constantinople minaret, laurel trees, and the top of Artur's carousel are lit by the last rays of the sun. The autumn sun is setting, sunset, sunset . . . KHLUDOV sits on the rug on the floor, legs folded under him in Turkish fashion, and talks to someone.

KHLUDOV: You have tormented me enough. But the darkness is lifting. Yes, lifting. But you must not forget that you are not the only one. There are the living, too, they hang around my neck, with their own demands. You see? Fate tied them into a single knot with me, and now I cannot pry them away. I have made peace with that. But one thing I cannot understand. You. How is it that you alone have separated yourself from the long chain of moons and lampposts? How did you get away from eternal peace? After all you were not the only one. Oh, no, there were many of you . . .

---

* From a Russian folk song.

88

(*Mutters.*) Well, remember me, remember me. But we shall not think of it. (*Broods, ages visibly, sags.*) Yes. And so I did it all for nothing. And what came after? Simply darkness—and we left. Then heat, and the carousel turning every day. But you, hunter! What a distance you have traveled after me, and now you've caught me, you've caught me in the sack! Don't torment me any more. Understand that I have made my decision, I swear to you. As soon as Golubkov returns, I'll go, at once. Come, ease my soul, nod to me. Nod at least once, eloquent orderly Krapilin! So! You did! It is decided!

SERAFIMA *enters noiselessly.*

SERAFIMA: What is it, Roman Valerianovich, again?

KHLUDOV: What? What?

SERAFIMA: To whom were you speaking? There is no one in the room but you!

KHLUDOV: It must have seemed to you. However, I have a habit of muttering. I hope it does not disturb anyone, eh?

SERAFIMA (*sits down on the rug near* KHLUDOV): I've lived here, behind the wall, four months, and at night I hear your muttering. Do you think it's easy? I cannot sleep myself on such nights. And now in the daytime too? Poor, poor man . . .

KHLUDOV: Very well. I shall get you another room, but on the same block, so I can keep an eye on you. I sold a ring, I have money. It is a bright room, with windows on the Bosphorus. Of course, I cannot offer any special comforts. You can see yourself—it's all nonsense. We're finished. We lost and were thrown out. And why did we lose, do you know? (*Points mysteriously over his shoulder.*) He and I know everything. It isn't too convenient for me either, to be living next to you, but I must keep my word.

SERAFIMA: Roman Valerianovich, do you remember the day when Golubkov left? You caught up with me and forced me to return, remember?

KHLUDOV: When someone's going out of his mind, you must use force. All of you are unhinged, somehow.

SERAFIMA: I suddenly felt sorry for you, Roman Valerianovich, that was the only reason I stayed.

KHLUDOV: I don't need a nursemaid, you need one!

SERAFIMA: Don't get irritated, you're only hurting yourself.

KHLUDOV: Yes, you're right, you're right. I can no longer hurt anyone. Do you remember—night, the head-quarters . . . Khludov the beast, Khludov the jackal? Eh?

SERAFIMA: All this is past, I have forgotten, don't recall it.

KHLUDOV (*mutters*): Yes, yes, yes . . . No, I am not allowed to forget. Remember, remember . . . However, let's not go back to it.

SERAFIMA: There you are, Roman Valerianovich. You know, I was thinking all night . . . We must make a decision what to do. How long can we sit here?

KHLUDOV: Wait till Golubkov returns, the tangle will unravel at once. I'll turn you over to him, and then it will be each for himself, we'll go our own ways. And that's that. A stifling city!

SERAFIMA: Ah, it was madness to let him go! I will never forgive myself! God, how I miss him! It was Lyuska's, Lyuska's fault . . . Her reproaches drove me out of my mind . . . Now I'm like you, I cannot sleep—he is surely lost now in his wanderings, he may be dead.

KHLUDOV: A stifling city! And that disgrace—the cockroach races! They all say I am deranged. Really, why did you let him go? There was something about money—your husband's money?

SERAFIMA: I have no husband! I forgot him, I curse him!

KHLUDOV: Well, then, in short, what's to be done?

SERAFIMA: Let's look the truth in the eyes: Sergey Pavlovich is gone, lost. And last night I made up my mind. The Cossacks were allowed to go home. I'll ask to go, too, I'll go back with them, to Petersburg. It was madness. Why did I ever leave?

KHLUDOV: Clever. Very. You are a clever woman, eh? You've never done anything against the Bolsheviks, you can safely return.

SERAFIMA: There is one thing, though, I don't know, one thing that keeps me here—what will become of you?

KHLUDOV (*beckons to her mysteriously; she moves nearer, and he speaks into her ear*): But shsh . . . for you it's nothing, but for me . . . the counter-intelligence is on my heels, they have a good nose . . . (*Whispers.*) I shall also return to Russia, we can go together. There is a ship leaving this very night.

SERAFIMA: You want to go secretly, under another name?

KHLUDOV: Under my own name. I'll come and say: I'm here—Khludov.

SERAFIMA: What are you saying? You'll be shot immediately!

KHLUDOV: Instantly. (*Smiles.*) On the spot. Eh? A cotton shirt, a cellar, snow . . . Done! My time's running out. Look, he walked away and stands there in the distance.

SERAFIMA: Ah! So that's what you mutter about! You want to die? Madman! Stay here, perhaps you will be cured?

KHLUDOV: I was cured today. I am entirely well. I'm not a cockroach, I won't swim in pails. I remember armies, battles, snow, lampposts, with lights on them . . . Khludov will walk under the lights.

A loud knocking on the door. It opens at once, and GOLUBKOV *and* CHARNOTA *enter. Both are dressed in good suits.* CHARNOTA *carries a small valise. Silence.*

SERAFIMA: Seryozha! Seryozha!

CHARNOTA: Hello! Why are you silent?

KHLUDOV: Well, here they are. They've come. I told you . . .

GOLUBKOV: Sima! Well, Sima!

SERAFIMA *embraces* GOLUBKOV, *crying.*

KHLUDOV (*wrinkling his face*): Come, Charnota, let's step out on the balcony and have a talk. (*They walk out behind the glass wall.*)

GOLUBKOV: There, don't cry, don't cry. Why are you crying, Serafima? I'm here, I'm back . . .

SERAFIMA: I thought you died! If you knew how I longed for you! . . . Now everything is clear to me . . . You're back! You'll never go away again, I won't let you.

GOLUBKOV: Of course not, never! All that is finished! And we'll decide everything right away. But how did you live here, Serafima, without me? Say something, a single word!

SERAFIMA: I am exhausted, I can't sleep. The moment you left, I came to my senses, I couldn't forgive myself for letting you go! I've sat up every night, looking at the lights outside, and seeing you in Paris, ragged, hungry . . . And Khludov is sick, he is so frightening!

GOLUBKOV: Don't, Serafima, don't!

SERAFIMA: You saw my husband?

GOLUBKOV: I did, I did. He has repudiated you, and he has a new wife—it doesn't matter who she is . . . And . . . it's better this way, and you are free! (*Shouts.*) Khludov, thanks!

KHLUDOV *and* CHARNOTA *enter.*

KHLUDOV: So, everything's all right now, eh? (*To* GOLUBKOV.) You love her? Eh? A sincere man? I advise you to go where she says. And now goodbye to you all! (*Takes his coat, hat, and a small valise.*)

CHARNOTA: Where to, if I may inquire?

KHLUDOV: There's a ship leaving tonight, I'm taking it. But keep it quiet.

GOLUBKOV: Roman! Think it over! You must not do it!

SERAFIMA: I spoke to him, you cannot hold him back.

KHLUDOV: Charnota! You know what? Come with me, eh?

CHARNOTA: Wait, wait, wait! I see it now! Where to? There? A fine idea! What is it all about? Some clever new plan? No wonder you were on the General Staff! Or are you going to face the reckoning? Eh? Then I can tell you, Roman, you will live exactly as long as it takes to get you off the boat and bring you to the nearest wall! And even then, under the heaviest guard, so you're not torn to pieces on the way! You've left quite a memory of yourself, brother. And, naturally, they won't leave me behind, they'll take me along for company, they will, they will . . . I've got plenty of sins to my name too! Though, to be sure, there were no lampposts!

SERAFIMA: Charnota! What are you saying to a sick man?

CHARNOTA: I'm saying it to stop him.

GOLUBKOV: Roman! Stay here, you cannot go!

KHLUDOV: You'll be homesick, Charnota.

CHARNOTA: Eh, tell me something new! I've been homesick for a long time, brother. Kiev won't let me rest, I keep remembering the monastery, the battles . . . I never ran from death, but I won't make a special trip for it, to the Bolsheviks. And I'm telling you, I'm sorry for you, don't go.

KHLUDOV: Well, goodbye! Goodbye! (*Leaves.*)

CHARNOTA: Serafima, stop him, he will regret it!

SERAFIMA: There's nothing I can do.

GOLUBKOV: You cannot hold him back, I know him.

CHARNOTA: Ah! The soul demands judgment! Well, then, there's nothing to be done! And you?

SERAFIMA: Let us go, Sergey, let's ask them. I've been thinking of it—let's go home tonight!

GOLUBKOV: Let us go, let us go! I am sick of wandering!

CHARNOTA: Oh, well, it's all right for you, they'll let you in. Let's divide up the money.

SERAFIMA: What money? Is it Korzukhin's money?

GOLUBKOV: He won twenty thousand dollars from Korzukhin in cards.

SERAFIMA: Never!

GOLUBKOV: And I don't need it either. I came here, and that's enough. We'll manage somehow to get to Russia. What you gave me will be enough.

CHARNOTA: I'm offering for the last time. No? Being noble? All right. And so, our ways are parting, fate divides us. One into the noose, others to Petersburg, and where do I go? Who am I now? From now on, I am the Wandering Jew! I'm Ahasuerus! The Flying Dutchman! I am the devil's dog!

The clock strikes five. In the distance, a flag is raised over the carousel. The sound of accordions and the chorus singing at Artur's races: "There were twelve brigands in the woods, and Kudeyar their chief . . ."

Bah! Do you hear? The jig's still there, it's going strong!

Flings open the door to the balcony. The sound of the chorus rises: "The brigands spilled a lot of blood of honest Christian men . . ."

Greetings to you again, Cockroach King Artur! You'll gasp when General Charnota appears before you in all his glory! (*Disappears.*)

GOLUBKOV: I cannot bear the sight of this city any more! I cannot bear to hear it!

SERAFIMA: What was it, Seryozha, what was it this past year and a half? Dreams? Tell me! Where, why did we run? Lampposts on the platform, black bags . . . then heat! I want to go back to Karavannaya, I want to see snow again! I want to forget everything, as if it never was!

The chorus swells: "Let us pray to the Lord and tell the ancient tale!" *From afar the muezzin's voice cries:* "La ilāha illa allāh . . ."

GOLUBKOV: No, nothing was, we dreamed it! Forget, forget it! A month will pass, we'll make our way, we'll get there, and then the snow will fall, it will cover our footprints . . . Come, come!

SERAFIMA: Come! It is over!

They run out of Khludov's room. Constantinople begins to fade and fades out forever.

Bliss

or The Dream of the Engineer Rein

A Play in Four Acts

CHARACTERS

Yevgeny Nikolayevich Rein, *an engineer*
Rein's Next-door Neighbor, *a woman*
Yury Miloslavsky, *alias The Actor*
Svyatoslav Vladimirovich Bunsha-Koretsky, *ex-prince, secretary of the House Management Committee*
Ivan the Terrible, *Tsar*
Henchman, *member of the Oprichina, or the tsar's guard*
Captain of the Tsar's Musketeers
Sergey Yevgenievich Mikhelson, *a citizen*
Pavel Sergeyevich Radamanov, *People's Commissar of Inventions*
Avrora, *his daughter*
Anna, *his secretary*
Ferdinand Savvich, *director of the Institute of Harmony*
Grabbe, *professor of medicine*
Guest
Obliging Guest
Militia Officer
Militiamen

The action takes place at different times.

ACT ONE

A *spring day. A Moscow apartment. Foyer with a telephone. Rein's large room, in total disorder. Next to it, the room of citizen Mikhelson, abundantly furnished.*

A *small mechanism on a table in Rein's room. Blueprints, instruments.* REIN, *in greasy overalls, unshaven, sleepless, works on the mechanism. From time to time, when* REIN *succeeds in setting it, distant musical sounds and muted noises begin to flow into the room.*

REIN: Three hundred and sixty-four . . . Same sound again . . . But nothing more . . .

Sudden excited voice of Rein's NEIGHBOR *offstage: "Herring . . . Last day . . ." Then muffled voices, footsteps, and someone knocking on Rein's door.*

All right, all right! Who is it now?

NEIGHBOR (*enters*): Sofya Petrovna! Sofya Pet . . . Oh, she's out? Comrade Rein, tell your wife the coop's selling herring today for the second coupon. Tell her to hurry up. This is the last day.

REIN: I cannot tell her anything, she went away last night.

NEIGHBOR: Where did she go?

REIN: To her lover.

NEIGHBOR: Isn't that something! What do you mean, her lover? What lover?

101

REIN: Who knows him! Some Pyotr Ivanovich, or Ilya Petrovich, I don't remember. All I know is that he wears a gray hat and is nonpartisan.

NEIGHBOR: Isn't that something! But you're an odd one! There's never been one like you in this house!

REIN: Excuse me, I am very busy.

NEIGHBOR: And what about the herring? Is that to go to waste?

REIN: I am very busy.

NEIGHBOR: And when is she coming home, from that . . . that nonpartisan fellow?

REIN: Never. She went to live with him.

NEIGHBOR: And you, I'll bet you're suffering?

REIN: Look, I am very busy.

NEIGHBOR: Well, well . . . What a business! See you . . . (Disappears.)

Muted voices backstage: "She left him . . . went to her lover . . . herring . . . the last day . . ." Then hurried footsteps, a slamming door, silence.

REIN: The bitches! (*Turns to his mechanism.*) Now, from the beginning. Patience. I'll take apart the whole row. (*Works.*)

The light gradually fades until Rein's room is in total darkness. Nothing but distant melodic sounds. The front door opens soundlessly and YURY MILOSLAVSKY *enters the foyer. He is well dressed, looks like an actor.*

MILOSLAVSKY (*listens at Rein's door*): Home. Everybody's at work, and this one's home. Fixing his gramophone. Which is Mikhelson's room? (*Reads the name plate on Mikhelson's door.*) Ah, here! Sergey Yevgenievich Mikhelson. What a peculiar lock. He must be sitting in his office and thinking: What a wonderful lock I've got on my door. But actually it's a piece of junk. (*He breaks open the lock and enters Mikhelson's room.*) Excellent furnishings. Bachelors always live well. I've noticed that. Ah, he has his own telephone too. A great convenience. Well, the first thing to do is to call him. (*On the telephone.*) People's Commissariat of Supply. Merci. Extension nine hundred. Merci. Comrade Mikhelson, please. Merci. (*Somewhat altering his voice.*) Comrade Mikhelson? Bonjour. Comrade Mikhelson, will you be at the office all day? Guess! An actress. No, we haven't met, but I'm dying to meet you. Until four? I'll call you again. I am very persistent. (*Puts down the receiver.*) He was terribly intrigued. Well, then, let's start. (*Breaks open the desk, selects the valuables, then goes on to the chests and the chiffonieres.*) Empire. A very neat man. (*Takes the clock off the wall, puts on Mikhelson's coat, tries on his hat.*) Just my size. But I'm a bit tired. (*Gets a carafe and some food from the sideboard, takes a drink.*) I wonder what he puts in his vodka. Delicious. No, it isn't wormwood. Such a cosy room. Likes to read. (*Takes a book from the table, reads.*) "Renowned and rich is Kochubey. His fields are boundless . . ."* Pretty verse. (*Speaks into the telephone.*) People's Commissariat of Supply. Merci. Extension nine hundred. Merci. Comrade Mikhelson. Merci. Comrade Mikhelson? It's me again. What do you put in your vodka? My name? That's a secret. What a surprise you'll have today! (*Puts down the receiver.*) Terribly mystified. (*Drinks.*) "Renowned and rich is Kochubey. His fields are boundless . . ."

* Opening lines of *Poltava*, a long poem by Pushkin.

Mikhelson's room fades, and Rein's room gradually brightens. A faintly glimmering ring of light appears around REIN *and his mechanism.*

REIN: Ah ha! It lights up. That's something else now.

A knocking at the door.

Ah, damn you all! Yes!

Extinguishes the ring of light. Enter BUNSHA-KORETSKY, *with a lady's hat on his head.*

I'm not home.

BUNSHA *smiles.*

Seriously, Svyatoslav Vladimirovich, I'm busy. What's that on your head?

BUNSHA: A hat.

REIN: Why don't you take a look at it?

BUNSHA (*at the mirror*): Lydia Vasilievna's! I must have put it on in her apartment.

REIN: You are an absent-minded man, Svyatoslav Vladimirovich. At your age a man should sit home and look after his grandchildren. And you're shuffling around the house all day with a notebook.

BUNSHA: I have no grandchildren. And if I stop going around, things will get completely out of hand.

REIN: The country will collapse?

BUNSHA: It will if people don't pay their rent.

REIN: I have no money, Svyatoslav Vladimirovich.

BUNSHA: A man cannot live without paying rent. In our house people think they can, but they can't. The people in our house! I cross the yard, and I shudder. All the windows are open, everybody is sprawled on the windowsills, talking about things that are forbidden to talk about altogether.

REIN: You ought to see a doctor, prince.

BUNSHA: Yevgeny Nikolayevich, I've proved conclusively that I am not a prince, so don't you call me prince.

REIN: You are a prince.

BUNSHA: No, I'm not a prince.

REIN: I don't understand your obstinacy. You are a prince.

BUNSHA: And I say I'm not. (*Takes out some papers.*) Here are the documents which certify that my mother was unfaithful to my father, and I am the son of our coachman Panteley. I even look like Panteley. Here, read it.

REIN: I wouldn't bother. So you are the coachman's son, but I have no money.

BUNSHA: I beg, pay your rent, or Lukovkin will have our house up on the delinquent board.

REIN: Yesterday my wife went off to some Pyotr Ilyich, then it's herrings, then this dilapidated relic a prince, or a coachman's son, the devil knows him, comes here and tortures me. My wife left me, you understand?

BUNSHA: Excuse me, but why didn't you report it to me?

REIN: What are you so upset about? Did you have designs on her too?

BUNSHA: Such designs that I must immediately make a record of her departure. Where did she go?

REIN: I wasn't curious enough to ask.

BUNSHA: Naturally, you weren't curious. But I am curious. I'll find out myself and enter it in the books. (*Pause.*) Ah. Let me sit down for a moment.

REIN: There's no need for you to sit down. How can I explain to you that I'm not to be disturbed when I'm working?

BUNSHA: No, try to explain it to me. The other day I heard a lecture, and I got a lot out of it. It was about venereal diseases. Our life is generally very interesting and useful nowadays, but in our house nobody understands that. We have a very peculiar house anyway. Take Mikhelson, for example. He keeps buying mahogany furniture, but when it comes to rent . . . And you've made a machine.

REIN: You are raving, Svyatoslav Vladimirovich!

BUNSHA: I appeal to you, Yevgeny Nikolayevich. Report your machine to the militia. It must be registered. They've been saying already in apartment fourteen that you're building an apparatus to fly away from the Soviet regime. And you know what that means—you'll be ruined, and I'll be taken along for company.

REIN: What swine said that?

BUNSHA: I beg your pardon, it was my niece.

REIN: Why are those devil's witches babbling all that nonsense? I know, it's your fault. You're an old pest. You creep around the house, spying on everybody, and then you go carrying tales—and all of them lies anyway!

BUNSHA: I am a man in an official position. It is my duty to observe. I am worried about this machine. I'll have to report it.

REIN: For God's sake, wait a while before you do anything. Very well, come over here. I am simply experimenting. I'm studying time. But how can I explain to you that time is a fiction, that there is no past and no future? . . . How can I explain to you the idea of space which can, for example, have five dimensions? But at least get one thing into your head—this is absolutely innocent and harmless. Nothing will explode. And, generally, it doesn't concern anybody in any way! Now take, for instance, minus-three sixty-four. Minus.

Let's switch it on. Minus—that's the past. (*He switches on the mechanism. The ring lights up. There is a melodious sound.*) Unfortunately, this is all. (*Switches it off. Pause.*) Ah, what an idiot I am! No, I am not an inventor, I'm a moron! The code is in reverse, and that means that I must turn on the plus! And if it's plus, then the figure must be reversed too! (*Rushes to the mechanism, turns a key and switches it on again.*)

The light in REIN's *room dims. A bell strikes. The wall dividing the room from Mikhelson's fades out and we see a palace chamber with vaulted ceilings.* IVAN THE TERRIBLE, *in a black monastic habit, with a staff in his hand, sits at a table dictating to his* HENCHMAN, *who wears a monk's robe over his rich brocade garments. From somewhere come the sounds of chanted prayers and the slow tolling of church bells.* REIN *and* BUNSHA *watch motionless.*

IVAN: . . . and to our spiritual adviser and guide . . .
HENCHMAN (*writes*): . . . guide . . .
IVAN: . . . to the Heavenly Kingdom, the Most Reverent Abbot Kozma, to whom . . .
HENCHMAN (*writes*): . . . Kozma, to whom . . .
IVAN: . . . and to our brethren in Christ . . . in Christ . . . Ivan Vasilievich, Tsar and Grand Duke of all the Russias . . .
HENCHMAN (*writes*): . . . of all the Russias . . .
IVAN: . . . offers his humble bows.
REIN: Ah!

Hearing his voice, IVAN *and his* HENCHMAN *turn their heads. The* HENCHMAN *jumps up with a wild cry, backs away, crossing himself repeatedly, and disappears.*

IVAN (*jumps up, making signs of the cross over himself and over* REIN): Avaunt! Alack, my sinful soul! Woe to me, wretch that I am! Accursed murderer! Oh-h! Avaunt! Avaunt thee! (*In a frenzy, he rushes into* REIN's *room, runs toward the door, crossing himself and the walls, and disappears in the hallway.*)

BUNSHA: So that's the kind of a machine you've devised, Yevgeny Nikolayevich!

REIN: That's Ivan the Terrible! Catch him! He'll be seen! Oh, God! Oh, God! (*Rushes out after* IVAN THE TERRIBLE.)

BUNSHA (*runs to the telephone in the foyer*): Militia? Officer on duty! This is the secretary of the house committee, Number Ten Bathhouse Lane. The physicist Rein in our house made a machine without permission, and a tsar came out of it! No, no, not I, the physicist Rein! Bathhouse Lane! Yes, I'm sober, I'm sober all right! Bunsha-Koretsky, yes, that's my name! I disclaim all responsibility! I'm willing to testify! We'll expect you, impatiently! (*Hangs up the receiver and hurries back to* REIN's *room.*)

REIN (*runs in*): There's no door to the roof in the attic, is there? Good Lord!

The tocsin rings out suddenly behind Ivan's palace chamber. A shot is heard. Shouts: Hey-ho! Hey-ho! *The* CAPTAIN OF THE TSAR'S MUSKETEERS *bursts into the chamber, carrying a halberd.*

CAPTAIN OF THE MUSKETEERS: Where is the Tsar?

BUNSHA: I don't know.

CAPTAIN OF THE MUSKETEERS (*crossing himself*): Infidel dogs! Hey-ho! Hey-ho! (*Swings his halberd.*)

REIN: What the devil! (*Runs to the apparatus and switches*

it off. The palace chamber and the CAPTAIN OF THE MUSKETEERS *vanish instantly, and the noise is silenced. The only thing that remains is a small dark gap in the wall of Mikhelson's room. Pause.*) Did you see it?

BUNSHA: I certainly did!

REIN: Wait a moment, did you just telephone?

BUNSHA: My word of honor, I didn't.

REIN: You old scoundrel! You just telephoned? I heard your nasty voice!

BUNSHA: You have no right . . .

REIN: If you said a single word, to anyone! . . . Ah, the devil with you! So he can't get out on the roof? Good God, if anyone sees him! He slammed the attic door, it's locked now! What luck they've all run off for those herrings!

At this moment MILOSLAVSKY, *alarmed by the noise, appears through the gap from Mikhelson's room. He has Mikhelson's clock under his arm.*

Now what!

MILOSLAVSKY: Sorry, I must have taken the wrong exit. What happened to the wall here? It seems to have collapsed. Excuse me, how do I get out into the street? Straight through? Merci.

REIN: No, no! Wait!

MILOSLAVSKY: I beg your pardon, what is it?

BUNSHA: Mikhelson's clock.

MILOSLAVSKY: Sorry, what Mikhelson's? This is my clock.

REIN (*to* BUNSHA): To hell with you and your clock! I guess I didn't turn the indicator down to zero. What the devil? (*To* MILOSLAVSKY.) What·period are you from? What's your name?

MILOSLAVSKY: Yury Miloslavsky.

REIN: It can't be!

MILOSLAVSKY: If you will pardon me, I have documents, but I left them in the country.

REIN: Who are you?

MILOSLAVSKY: Why do you want to know? Oh, well, I am an actor. I'm with the state theaters.

REIN: I don't understand anything. Do you belong to our own period? Then how did you come out of the apparatus?

BUNSHA: And Mikhelson's coat.

MILOSLAVSKY: If you pardon me, why Mikhelson's? Is Mikhelson the only man in Moscow with a coat of fine covert cloth?

REIN: Oh, to the devil with you and your coat! (*Looks at the dial on the mechanism.*) Of course! I stopped it three years short of today. Be so kind, step over here, and I will send you back. (*Tries to turn the dial.*) What's wrong now? The needle is stuck! Wouldn't you know! Good God! And there's the other one up in the attic! (*To* MILOSLAVSKY.) Don't worry, please. Let me explain it to you. I have invented a time machine, and you've been carried . . . In short, don't get alarmed. I'll . . . I'll have it all straightened out in a moment. The point is that time is a fiction . . .

MILOSLAVSKY: You don't say! It never occurred to me to look at it that way!

REIN: That's the whole point. And the machine, you see . . .

MILOSLAVSKY: A rich article! But pardon me, what is this? A gold key?

REIN: Yes, gold. One moment, I'll just get the screwdriver.

He turns away. MILOSLAVSKY *bends over the machine. The glowing ring suddenly flares up, the light in the room changes, and a violent wind sweeps through the room.*

What's this? Who touched the machine?

BUNSHA: Help! (*The wind catches up* BUNSHA, *sweeps him into the ring of light, and he disappears.*)

MILOSLAVSKY: Oh, damn! (*He grabs at the curtain, pulls it off, is sucked into the ring and disappears.*)

REIN: What could have happened? (*He flies into the ring and seizes the machine.*) The key! The key! Where is the key? (*Disappears together with the machine.*)

Total silence in the house. After a long pause the front door opens and MIKHELSON *enters.*

MIKHELSON (*at the door to his room*): Merciful heavens! (*Enters the room.*) Merciful heavens! (*Rushes frantically back and forth.*) Heavens, heavens! (*Rushes to the telephone.*) Militia! Militia! Bathhouse Lane, Number Ten . . . What tsar? There is no tsar, I've been robbed! Mikhelson, Mikhelson's my name! (*Throws down the receiver.*) Good Heavens!

Impatient ringing at the front door. MIKHELSON *opens the door and several* MILITIAMEN *enter.*

Thank God, comrades! How did you make it so fast?

MILITIAMEN: Where is the tsar?

MIKHELSON: What tsar? I've been robbed! They broke through the wall! Take a look! My clock, my coat, my suits! My cigarette case! Everything I owned in the world!

MILITIA OFFICER: Who telephoned about the tsar?

MIKHELSON: What tsar are you talking about, comrades? They've robbed me! Take a look!

MILITIA OFFICER: No panic, citizen! Comrade Sidorov, cover the back stairs.

MIKHELSON: Robbed!

Darkness. And now we see the part of Moscow which is called Bliss. A spacious, columned terrace at a great height above ground. Marble everywhere. An unobtrusive but complex apparatus, unknown in our time. RADAMANOV, *the People's Commissar of Inventions, sits at a table in a house jacket, reading. A vast sky spreads over Bliss; a vivid spring sunset.*

ANNA (*enters*): Pavel Sergeyevich, what are you doing?

RADAMANOV: Reading.

ANNA: It's time for you to dress. The signal will be given in fifteen minutes.

RADAMANOV (*takes out his watch*): Ah! Is Avrora back?

ANNA: She is. (*Exits.*)

AVRORA (*enters*): Yes, I'm back. Best wishes to you on May Day.

RADAMANOV: Thank you. The same to you. By the way, Savvich called nine times today while you were away.

AVRORA: He's in love with me, and it's fun to torment him.

RADAMANOV: But don't you two torment me! He started ringing at eight in the morning to ask if you were back.

AVRORA: What do you think, papa, shall I make him happy or not?

RADAMANOV: Frankly, I don't care. But at least give him an answer today, whatever it may be.

AVRORA: You know, papa, I think I've become a little disillusioned with him.

RADAMANOV: I remember, just a month ago you were standing by that column and taking up my time telling me how much you liked Savvich.

AVRORA: I may have imagined something for a moment. But now I don't see what I could have liked about him. Was it his eyebrows? Or did he impress me with his theory of harmony? Harmony, papa . . .

RADAMANOV: Sorry. But if you can dispense with it, please don't talk to me about harmony. I've heard all about it from Savvich . . .

A blue light flashes in the apparatus on the table.

There he is, if you please. (*Into the apparatus.*) Yes, yes, she is here.

The light goes out.

He'll be up in a moment. I beg you, get the business done with, one way or the other. I am going to dress. (*Exits.*)

A trap door opens and SAVVICH *appears. He is dazzlingly dressed in an evening coat and carries a bunch of flowers in his hand.*

SAVVICH: My dear Avrora, don't be surprised. I've only dropped in for a moment, before the guests arrive. Permit me to give you these flowers.

AVRORA: Thank you. Sit down, Ferdinand.

SAVVICH: Avrora, I've come for an answer. You said you would give me an answer tonight.

AVRORA: Oh, yes, yes. This is May Day eve. You know what, let's postpone our conversation till midnight. I want to get things sorted out in my mind.

SAVVICH: I obey. I am ready to wait till midnight, although I am certain that nothing can change in these few hours. Believe me, Avrora, our union is inevitable. We are a harmonious pair. And I shall do everything in my power to make you happy.

AVRORA: Thank you, Ferdinand.

SAVVICH: And so, allow me to bid you good-bye. I shall be here as soon as the celebration begins.

AVRORA: We shall be glad to see you.

SAVVICH *exits.* RADAMANOV *enters, half dressed.*

RADAMANOV: He's gone?

AVRORA: He's gone.

RADAMANOV: You sent him off without an answer again?

AVRORA: Like every attractive woman, I am a bit capricious.

RADAMANOV: If you will pardon me, you are not at all as attractive as you think. What are you doing to the man?

AVRORA: On the other hand, of course, eyebrows aren't everything. A man may have the most insignificant eyebrows, and yet be an interesting man.

Clatter of broken glass backstage. The light goes out and flashes on, and BUNSHA *comes flying onto the terrace, followed by* MILOSLAVSKY *and, finally,* REIN.

REIN: Oh, God!

BUNSHA: Yevgeny Nikolayevich!

MILOSLAVSKY: Where am I now?

RADAMANOV: Actors. But why break my windows? And don't you know that film makers must give advance notice? This is my apartment.

REIN: Where are we? Will you please tell us where we are?

AVRORA: In Bliss.

RADAMANOV: Excuse me . . .

AVRORA: Wait, papa. This is a carnival joke. They're in costumes.

RADAMANOV: In the first place, it's too early. And in the second place, after all, the terrace windows . . .

There's a lady's hat on one of them. This may be very clever, but . . .

REIN: This is Moscow? (*Runs to the railing, looks down on the city.*) Ah! (*Turns with a stunned face, looks at the luminous calendar.*) Four twos. The year two thousand, two hundred, and twenty-two! Everything is clear! We are in the twenty-third century. (*Faints.*)

AVRORA: Wait! He really fainted! He hurt his head! Father! Anna! Anna! (*Rushes to* REIN.)

ANNA *runs in.*

RADAMANOV (*into the apparatus*): Doctor Grabbe! Come up here, please! Yes! Come as you are! There's something fantastic here! He hurt his head!

ANNA: Who are these people?

AVRORA: Water!

BUNSHA: Is he dead?

The trap opens and GRABBE, *half-dressed, runs in.*

AVRORA: Here, Professor, here!

GRABBE *revives* REIN.

REIN (*coming to*): Listen to me . . . But please believe me . . . I invented a machine for traveling in time . . . There it is . . . Try to understand me . . . We are men of the twentieth century!

Darkness.

ACT TWO

Night. The same terrace. Bright illumination. A buffet with champagne. RADAMANOV *and* REIN, *in evening coats, stand near the communication apparatus.* SAVVICH, *some distance away.* ANNA, *in evening dress, near the apparatus. Powerful strains of music.*

RADAMANOV: Over there, where the Bliss district ends, you see glass towers. That is the Azure Vertical. Now look—you see that swarm of lights? Those are the residents of the Vertical, flying here.
REIN: Yes, yes.

A light flashes in the apparatus.

ANNA: The Azure Vertical wants to see the engineer Rein.
RADAMANOV: You don't mind?
REIN: No, with pleasure.
ANNA (*into the apparatus*): You will now hear the People's Commissar of Inventions, Radamanov.
RADAMANOV (*to* REIN): Will you step here, please. (*Speaks into the apparatus, light falling upon him from above.*) Greetings to the Azure Vertical on May Day!

A swarm of fireflies sweeps past the terrace. REIN *is suddenly flooded with light from above.*

You wanted to see Rein? There he is before you. An

engineer of genius, Rein, a man of the twentieth century who has penetrated time! All the reports are true! There he is! Yevgeny Rein!

A *humming sound. The fireflies disappear.*

Look at the excitement you've caused in the world.

The apparatus lights go out.

But you are probably tired.

REIN: Oh, no! I want to see everything. No, the real genius is your Doctor Grabbe. I am full of energy. He blew the breath of life into me.

SAVVICH: That medicine should not be abused.

RADAMANOV: Have you met?

REIN: Not yet.

RADAMANOV: Savvich, director of the Institute of Harmony. Engineer Rein. (*To* REIN.) Perhaps, you'd like to see the dancing? Anna, will you entertain our guest and take him to the other rooms?

ANNA: With the greatest of pleasure.

ANNA *and* REIN *exit. Pause.*

RADAMANOV: Well, what will you say to all this, my dear Ferdinand?

SAVVICH: I am astounded. I don't understand anything. (*Pause.*) Tell me, Pavel Sergeyevich, what can possibly be the consequences of it all?

RADAMANOV: My dear, I am not a prophet. (*Pats his pockets.*) Do you have a cigarette? I seem to have mislaid my cigarette case in all this excitement.

SAVVICH (*pats his pockets*): Imagine that, I've left mine behind too. (*Pause.*) Radamanov! But it's impossible!

RADAMANOV: Well, now, that's a new one. How can a thing that is be impossible? No, my dear Ferdinand, no, my dear worshipper of harmony, you'll have to reconcile yourself to the idea. Three men have dropped on us from the fourth dimension. Well? We shall live, we shall see. Ah, I'm dying for a smoke. (*Both exit.*)

The sound of applause. Enter BUNSHA *and behind him, backing in, bowing to someone,* MILOSLAVSKY. *Both are freshly shaven and in evening coats.*

MILOSLAVSKY: Delighted, delighted. Merci, grand merci. Another time, with pleasure. Merci. (*To* BUNSHA.) They like us.

BUNSHA: All this is pretty queer. Socialism isn't meant for having fun. And here they're giving balls. And saying such things—uh-uh . . . And the main thing, those evening coats. Wouldn't they give 'em hell for those evening coats!

MILOSLAVSKY: One close look at you is enough to disillusion a man. Who'd give them hell?

Enter a GUEST *in an evening coat.*

GUEST: I understand, you want to be alone. I'll leave in a moment. I only wanted to shake hands with the companions of the great Rein.

MILOSLAVSKY: Delighted, delighted. Merci, grand merci. Miloslavsky, Yury. And this is our secretary. And may I ask who you may be?

GUEST: I am the superintendent of the Moscow water supply station.

MILOSLAVSKY: Very pleased. So you are also a working man. No, handshakes are not enough. We must embrace.

GUEST: I'll be happy and honored.

MILOSLAVSKY *embraces the* GUEST.

GUEST: I shall never forget this moment. (*Wants to embrace* BUNSHA.)
MILOSLAVSKY: It's not necessary with him. He's the secretary . . .
GUEST: My very, very best wishes to you. Good bye. (GUEST *exits.*)
MILOSLAVSKY: What pleasant people! Simple, trusting, without pretensions.
BUNSHA: He ought to come to a general meeting in that evening coat! I'd like to see that! I'd be interested to know his class origins.
MILOSLAVSKY: Will you stop buzzing in my ears! You don't let me figure things out.
BUNSHA: I've figured it all out already. In fact, I'll be glad to tell you what I think. But there's one thing I can't understand: where did you get a clock just like Mikhelson's? I'm beginning to entertain certain suspicions. (*Approaches the table on which the things brought from the twentieth century are laid out: the clock, a curtain, a lady's hat.*) There's even a name scratched out on it—"Mikhelson."
MILOSLAVSKY: I scratched it out myself.
BUNSHA: But why scratch out somebody else's name?
MILOSLAVSKY: Because I liked it. It's a beautiful name. All right, I'll rub it off and scratch out a new name: Miloslavsky. Does that reassure you?
BUNSHA: No, it does not reassure me. I have my suspicions anyway.
MILOSLAVSKY: Oh, God! What a bore! What would I, a prosperous man, want with Mikhelson's very mediocre

clock? Now here is a watch that's really something! (*Takes a watch from his pocket.*)

BUNSHA: Comrade Radamanov has a watch just like it . . . and the letter "R" . . .

MILOSLAVSKY: There, you see now.

BUNSHA: And you treat me much too familiarly, anyway.

MILOSLAVSKY: You can treat me familiarly too.

ANNA (*enters*): You aren't bored here by yourselves? Let's have some champagne.

MILOSLAVSKY: Thank you most humbly. But forgive me, mademoiselle, for an immodest question. Could we possibly have some plain alcohol instead—as an exception?

ANNA: Alcohol? You drink alcohol?

MILOSLAVSKY: How can a man refuse?

ANNA: Oh, how interesting! But, unfortunately, we don't serve alcohol. But there's that faucet, you can get pure alcohol from it.

MILOSLAVSKY: Your apartments are certainly equipped with every convenience! Bunsha, a glass!

ANNA: Isn't it too fiery?

MILOSLAVSKY: Try it. Bunsha, a glass for the lady.

ANNA (*drinks down*): Oh!

MILOSLAVSKY: Chase it down with a bite of food.

BUNSHA: Yes, a bite of food!

At this moment the GUEST comes in. Diffidently, trying to be unobtrusive, he looks for something under the table.

MILOSLAVSKY: What are you looking for, my good man?

GUEST: Sorry, I dropped a locket and a chain somewhere . . .

MILOSLAVSKY: Oh-h, that's a pity.

GUEST: Excuse me, I'll take a look in the ballroom again. (*Exits.*)

MILOSLAVSKY: What charming people you have here. Your health! Another glass!

ANNA: I won't get drunk?

MILOSLAVSKY: On alcohol? Not on your life. But have some hors d'oeuvres with it. Prince, this is an excellent pâté.

BUNSHA: Didn't I tell you about Panteley?

MILOSLAVSKY: To the devil with you and your Panteley! They don't give a damn who you are. Your origin is unimportant here.

BUNSHA (*to* ANNA): Permit me to inquire, comrade, what union you belong to.

ANNA: Sorry, I don't know what you mean.

BUNSHA: I mean, to put it in a different way, where do you pay your dues?

ANNA (*laughing*): I still don't understand.

MILOSLAVSKY: You're disgracing me, Bunsha. You'll be asking about the militia next. They don't have anything of the kind.

BUNSHA: No militia? Oh, no, you're making that up. Where are they going to register us if there's no militia?

ANNA: Forgive me for smiling, but I can't understand a single word you're saying. Who were you in your past life?

BUNSHA: I am the secretary of the house management committee in our building.

ANNA: And . . . and . . . what do you do in that post?

BUNSHA: I take care of the cards, comrade.

ANNA: Oh. Is it interesting work? How do you spend your day?

BUNSHA: Very interesting. In the morning I get up and have my tea. Then the wife goes off to the co-op, and I sit down to fill out the cards. First of all I see whether anyone died in the house. If he died, I immediately void his card.

ANNA (*laughs gaily*): I don't understand a thing.

MILOSLAVSKY: Allow me to explain. In the morning he gets up and begins to write out the cards. He registers the living and signs out the dead. Then he distributes the cards. A week later he collects them and writes out new ones. Then he distributes them again, then he collects them again, and writes out new ones . . .

ANNA (*laughing loudly*): You're joking! But that's enough to drive you crazy!

MILOSLAVSKY: He's crazy.

ANNA: I am dizzy. I am drunk. You told me alcohol doesn't make you drunk.

MILOSLAVSKY: Permit me to support you. (*Puts an arm around her waist.*)

ANNA: Certainly. Your approach to a woman seems gallant, but it's somewhat strange in our day. Tell me, were you Rein's assistant?

MILOSLAVSKY: Not so much an assistant as an intimate friend, so to speak. In fact, not even his friend, but his neighbor's, Mikhelson's. I happened to be passing by in the streetcar and I thought, why not drop in? And Zhenya says to me . . .

ANNA: Rein?

MILOSLAVSKY: Rein, yes, Rein. He says, let's take a little trip, shall we? And so I said, why not? Let's . . . (*To* BUNSHA.) Keep quiet a minute. And so, here we are. That's the story . . . Permit me to kiss your hand.

ANNA: Certainly. I adore brave men.

MILOSLAVSKY: In our profession, you can't be timid. Lose your nerve, and you have five years to repent in.

RADAMANOV (*enters*): Anna dear, I've lost my watch somewhere in all this excitement.

MILOSLAVSKY: I didn't see it.

ANNA: I'll look for it later.

BUNSHA: Comrade Radamanov . . .

RADAMANOV: Yes?

BUNSHA: Comrade Radamanov, I'd like to submit my documents to you.

RADAMANOV: What documents?

BUNSHA: So you can register us. Here we are enjoying ourselves at your ball, and we're still unregistered. I consider it my duty to bring it to your attention.

RADAMANOV: Sorry, my dear man, I don't know what you mean . . . If you don't mind, let's talk about it later . . . (*Exits.*)

BUNSHA: What a lax apparatus. You can't get anywhere with anybody.

GRABBE (*enters*): Ah, at last I found you! Radamanov is worried that you may be tired after your flight. (*To* ANNA.) Excuse me, one moment. (*Bends over* MILO-SLAVSKY's *chest, listens to his heart.*) Did you drink anything?

MILOSLAVSKY: Lemonade.

GRABBE: Well, everything's in order. (*To* BUNSHA.) And you?

BUNSHA: My back hurts in the evening, comrade doctor, and my stool is very hard.

GRABBE: We'll take care of it, we'll take care of it. Allow me, your pulse. But where's my watch? Could I have dropped it?

MILOSLAVSKY: You must have dropped it.

GRABBE: It doesn't matter. Good bye. Could I have left it in my coat? (*Exits.*)

ANNA: What is this? Everybody seems to have gone crazy with their watches.

MILOSLAVSKY: It's a scream! An epidemic!

BUNSHA (*to* MILOSLAVSKY, *in an undertone*): Mikhelson's clock—one. Radamanov's watch—two. This latest unexplained case . . . My suspicions are growing . . .

MILOSLAVSKY: You make me sick. (*To* ANNA.) Shall we take a walk?

ANNA: I can hardly stand after your alcohol.

MILOSLAVSKY: Lean on me. (*To* BUNSHA, *in an undertone.*) Why don't you go somewhere else? Go on, have your fun on your own. What are you tagging after me for? (*The three exit.*)

Enter REIN *and* AVRORA. REIN *is clutching his head.*

AVRORA: My dear Yevgeny Nikolayevich, but where is he?

REIN: One of the two: he's either still in the attic, or he was captured. Most likely, he is already locked up in a psychiatric ward. You know, whenever I think of it, my hair stands up on end. Yes, yes . . . Yes . . . I'm sure the militia have caught up with him already. I can imagine what's going on there! But then, it's useless to talk about it now. There's nothing to be done, anyway.

AVRORA: Stop worrying. Better have some wine.

REIN: You're quite right. (*Drinks.*) Such a business . . .

AVRORA: I look at you, and I cannot tear myself away. Do you realize what kind of a man you are? My dear, dear Rein, when do you expect to repair your machine?

REIN: Oh, you know, I'm in trouble there. I've lost an important part. But we'll see about it . . .

Pause.

AVRORA: Tell me about your life. Were you married?

REIN: Of course.

AVRORA: And.what about your wife now?

REIN: She ran away from me.

AVRORA: From you? To whom?

REIN: To some Semyon Petrovich, I don't know exactly . . .

AVRORA: But why did she leave you?

REIN: I spent everything on the machine, I couldn't even pay the rent.

AVRORA: Ah, ah . . . And you . . .

REIN: What?

AVRORA: No, nothing, nothing.

The clock strikes midnight. Sounds from the ballroom. The hatch opens and SAVVICH *appears.*

AVRORA: It's midnight. Ah, there's my fiance.

REIN: Ah!

AVRORA: You've met?

SAVVICH: I've had the pleasure.

AVRORA: You wish to talk to me, Ferdinand, don't you?

SAVVICH: If I may. I've come at midnight, as you said.

REIN: Please, please, I . . . (*Gets up.*)

AVRORA: Don't go far, Rein, we have only a few words to say. (REIN *exits.*) My dear Ferdinand, you have come for your answer?

SAVVICH: Yes.

AVRORA: Don't be angry at me, and try to forget me. I cannot be your wife.

Pause.

SAVVICH: Avrora, Avrora! But this cannot be. What are you doing? We were born for each other.

AVRORA: No, Ferdinand, this is a sad mistake. We were not born for each other.

SAVVICH: Tell me one thing: has anything happened?

AVRORA: Nothing has happened. I've simply taken a good look at myself, and I see that I am not the woman for you. Believe me, Ferdinand, you were mistaken when you thought we were a harmonious pair.

SAVVICH: I am convinced that you will change your mind, Avrora. The Institute of Harmony does not make mistakes, I shall prove it to you! (*Exits.*)

AVRORA: Such faith in harmony! (*Calls.*) Rein!

REIN *enters.*

Forgive me, please. Well, now, the conversation is over. Pour me some wine, please. Let's go back to the ballroom.

REIN *and* AVRORA *exit.*

MILOSLAVSKY (*backs in*): No, merci. Grand merci. (*Clears his throat.*) I am not in good voice today. Really, I'm not. I thank you, I thank you most kindly.

ANNA (*runs in*): If you recite, I'll give you a kiss.

MILOSLAVSKY: I accept the condition. (*Holds out his face.*)

ANNA: When you finish. And you lied about the alcohol— it's terribly strong.

MILOSLAVSKY: My apologies . . .

RADAMANOV (*enters*): I beg you, do me a favor, recite something for my guests.

MILOSLAVSKY: But, Pavel Sergeyevich, I only recite poetry. I have no repertory to speak of.

RADAMANOV: Poetry? But that's excellent. I'll be frank with you, I don't know anything about poetry, but I am certain that everyone will be most delighted.

ANNA: Please come to the apparatus. We shall broadcast you to all the rooms.

MILOSLAVSKY: I'm very shy, that's my trouble . . .

ANNA: Doesn't look like it.

A spotlight falls on MILOSLAVSKY.

(*She speaks into the apparatus.*) Attention! The twentieth century actor Yury Miloslavsky will now recite poetry. (*Applause in the apparatus.*) Whose poetry will you recite?

MILOSLAVSKY: What did you say? Oh, my own.

Applause in the apparatus. The same GUEST *enters. He is extremely gloomy and looks down at the floor.*

Renowned . . . and rich . . . is Kochubey . . . Uhm . . . His fields . . . are boundless!

ANNA: Go on!

MILOSLAVSKY: That's all.

A puzzled silence, followed by applause.

RADAMANOV: Bravo, bravo . . . Thank you.

MILOSLAVSKY: Not a bad little poem, is it?

RADAMANOV: No, but a bit short, somehow. However, I consider that a virtue in poetry. Our people make their poems much longer.

MILOSLAVSKY: Oh, well, sorry I didn't please.

RADAMANOV: Oh, no, oh, no . . . I repeat, I know nothing about poetry. Your audience is enthusiastic—listen to that applause.

Shouts in the apparatus. "Miloslavsky! Yury!"

ANNA: Come and take a bow.

MILOSLAVSKY: What's that for? I'm shy . . .

ANNA: Come on, come on.

ANNA *and* MILOSLAVSKY *exit. Sounds of a stormy ovation.*

RADAMANOV (*to the* GUEST): What's the matter with you, my friend? Are you ill?

GUEST: No, no, it's nothing.

RADAMANOV: Have some champagne. (*Exits.*)

GUEST (*alone, drinks down three glasses, then gets down on all fours and crawls about on the floor for a while, looking for something.*) Stupid verses . . . Who's that Kochubey? Can't make head or tail of it . . . Disgusting writing . . . (*Exits.*)

An OBLIGING GUEST *runs in, turns on the light in the apparatus.*

OBLIGING GUEST: Philharmonic? Be so kind, find the record called "Hallelujah." Do it right away and put it on, transmit it to Radamanov's reception hall. It's the only music the actor Miloslavsky will dance to . . . A prayer? Just a moment . . . (*Runs out, comes back.*) No, not a prayer, a dance. Late nineteen-twenties. (*The first strains of "Hallelujah" are heard in the apparatus.* OBLIGING GUEST *hurries out, returns a few moments later.*) That's it! (*Runs out.*)

REIN *and* AVRORA *enter.*

AVRORA: No one here. That's good. I'm tired of the crowd.

REIN: Shall I see you to your room?

AVRORA: No, I want to be with you.

REIN: What did you tell your fiance?

AVRORA: That does not concern you.

REIN: What did you tell your fiance?

AVRORA *suddenly embraces* REIN *and kisses him.*

BUNSHA *appears.*

REIN: You always come in at the wrong time, Svyatoslav Vladimirovich!

BUNSHA *disappears.*

OBLIGING GUEST (*runs in, speaks into the apparatus*): Louder! Much louder! (*Runs out, then returns and speaks into the apparatus.*) He says, with bells! Give us the bells! (*Runs out, then returns and speaks into the apparatus.*) And cannon shots! (*Runs out.*)

Thunderous sounds of "Hallelujah" with cannon shots and bells.

OBLIGING GUEST (*returns*): That's it. Continue. (*Runs out.*)

REINS Has he gone mad? (*Hurries out with* AVRORA.)

Darkness.

ACT THREE

The same terrace. Early morning. REIN, *in his overalls, over his mechanism. He is troubled. Tries to recall something.* AVRORA *comes in on tiptoe and watches him silently.*

REIN: No, I can't remember, I'll never remember it . . .

AVRORA: Rein! (*He turns around.*) Don't torment yourself. Take a rest.

REIN: Avrora! (*They kiss.*)

AVRORA: Admit it, you were up all night again?

REIN: All right, I was.

AVRORA: Don't dare to work at night. You'll simply wear yourself out. You'll lose your memory and won't get anywhere. Even I—I woke three times last night . . . I keep dreaming of figures and figures . . .

REIN: Sh-sh . . . I thought I heard steps . . .

AVRORA: Who'd come without a signal? (*Pause.*) You know, I am obsessed with the idea of our flying away together. Whenever I think of it, my mind reels . . . I want flight, I want danger! Rein, do you realize what kind of a man you are!

Light in the communication apparatus.

It's father. His signal. Let's fly off somewhere. You need a rest.

REIN: I must change.

AVRORA: Nonsense! Let's go! (*They exit.*)

RADAMANOV *enters, stops near* REIN's *machine, looks at it for a long time, then sits down at his desk and rings.*

ANNA (*enters*): Good morning, Pavel Sergeyevich!

RADAMANOV: Well?

ANNA: I cannot find them, Pavel Sergeyevich. They aren't anywhere. They've simply disappeared.

RADAMANOV: What do you mean, disappeared? That would be in the realm of magic altogether.

ANNA: Pavel Sergeyevich, the Lost and Found Office looked for them.

RADAMANOV: What has the Lost and Found to do with it? The watch and the cigarette case were in my pocket.

ANNA: Believe me, Pavel Sergeyevich, I am so upset about it . . .

RADAMANOV: Well, if you're upset, to the devil with it! Don't look anymore!

ANNA *walks toward the door.*

By the way, how is that . . . Yury Miloslavsky?

ANNA: I don't know, Pavel Sergeyevich. Why did you think of him?

RADAMANOV: I really don't know. But somehow, the moment I think of the watch, I immediately think of his poem about that—what's his name?—Kochubey . . . Is it a good poem?

ANNA: It's an ancient poem, of course, but it's good. And he recites magnificently, Pavel Sergeyevich!

RADAMANOV: Well, so much the better. Very well.

ANNA *exits.* RADAMANOV *becomes absorbed in his work. A signal flashes on the table, but* RADAMANOV *does not notice it.* SAVVICH *enters, stops silently, and looks at* RADAMANOV.

RADAMANOV (*reads a while longer without noticing him, then mechanically puts his hand in his pocket.*) Renowned and rich . . . (*Sees* SAVVICH.) Ah!

SAVVICH: I rang. Your door was open.

RADAMANOV: I didn't notice. Sit down, please. (*Pause.*) You don't look too well. (*Pause.*) Have you come to be silent with me?

SAVVICH: No, Radamanov, I've come to speak to you.

RADAMANOV: Oh-h . . . oh . . . You must agree, my dear Ferdinand, it's not my fault that I'm her father . . . and . . . let's consider the subject closed. Shall we have some coffee?

SAVVICH: Beware those three who've come here!

RADAMANOV: Are you trying to scare me early in the morning?

SAVVICH: Beware of them!

RADAMANOV: What do you want, my dear? Express yourself more clearly.

SAVVICH: I want them to get the hell out of here!

RADAMANOV: Everybody says unanimously that hell does not exist, Ferdinand. Besides, all this is not so simple. In fact, my friend, it's quite the opposite . . .

SAVVICH: You mean, they're to remain here?

RADAMANOV: Exactly.

SAVVICH: Ah, I see. I realize the importance of this machine. Your commissariat may be concerned with saving the invention for our century, but the Institute of Harmony must see to it that those three aliens don't disrupt life in Bliss! And they will not disrupt it, I promise you! I shall protect our people and, most of all, I shall protect her whom I consider the finest adornment of Bliss—Avrora! You don't appreciate her enough! Goodbye! (*Exits.*)

RADAMANOV: Oh-h . . . oh . . . What a business . . . (*Rings.*)

ANNA *enters*.

Please switch off all signals. I don't want to see anyone.
ANNA: Yes. (*Exits.*)

A *little later* BUNSHA *appears. He sits down silently
where* SAVVICH *sat before.*

RADAMANOV (*raising his head*): What now! My dear man,
why didn't you ring before coming up?
BUNSHA: It's a very convenient apparatus, but I pulled and
pulled the handle . . .
RADAMANOV: Why pull it? It's switched off.
BUNSHA: Oh.
RADAMANOV: Well, what can I do for you?
BUNSHA (*hands him a sheet of paper*): I have a complaint,
Comrade Radamanov.
RADAMANOV: First of all, Svyatoslav Vladimirovich, let's
not have any papers. This isn't our custom, as I've told
you five times. We avoid papers in every way we can.
Just tell me about it in plain words. That's simpler,
quicker, more convenient. Well, then, what is your
complaint?
BUNSHA: I want to complain against the Institute of Har-
mony.
RADAMANOV: How did it displease you?
BUNSHA: I want to get married.
RADAMANOV: To whom?
BUNSHA: To anyone.
RADAMANOV: The first time I hear such a thing. And . . .
BUNSHA: And it's the job of the Institute of Harmony to
find me a wife.
RADAMANOV: My dearest friend, what are you saying! The

Institute is not a matchmaker, The Institute studies the human race, it is concerned with its purity, it strives to bring about ideal selection, but it doesn't interfere in marital relations except in extreme cases when they threaten harm to our society.

BUNSHA: And is it a classless society?

RADAMANOV: You've guessed it at once—it is classless.

BUNSHA: All over the world?

RADAMANOV: Definitely, all over. (*Pause.*) I see that something troubles you in my reply.

BUNSHA: It does, Comrade Radamanov. I detect some sort of a deviation in your words.

RADAMANOV: Would you mind explaining it to me? I don't understand what deviation means.

BUNSHA: I'll explain to you all about deviations sometime, on a day off. But think about it, Pavel Sergeyevich, and be careful in your theories.

RADAMANOV: I shall be very grateful to you, but let's return to our problem. You'll have to find yourself a wife on your own. And if the Institute of Harmony raises any obstacles in your way, as a man who is a newcomer here, we shall talk about it then.

BUNSHA: Pavel Sergeyevich, in our transitional period I knew how to talk to ladies. But in a classless society . . .

RADAMANOV: It's done exactly as in a class society.

BUNSHA: What would you say to her?

RADAMANOV: I wouldn't say anything, my good man, not for the world. I lost my wife a long time ago, and I haven't the least inclination for family life. But if such a silly fancy came into my head, I'd say something like: "I've fallen in love with you at first sight . . . And you seem to like me too . . ." Excuse me, I cannot talk any more, I am expected at a meeting. Why don't you talk it over with Anna or Avrora, they're better equipped than I . . . A good day to you. (*Exits.*)

BUNSHA: A fine fellow, not a bureaucrat. Just one of the boys. A man to be prized and cherished. (*Sits down at* RADAMANOV'*s desk and rings.*)

ANNA (*enters*): Yes, Pavel Ser . . . Was it you who rang?

BUNSHA: I rang.

ANNA: Most interesting. Was there anything you wished to tell me?

BUNSHA: I fell in love with you at first sight.

ANNA: I am very flattered, I'm really touched, but unfortunately my heart is occupied. (*Puts a paper on the desk.*)

BUNSHA: No need for papers, I've said this before, time and again. Just tell it to me in plain words. It's faster, simpler, and more convenient. Do you refuse me?

ANNA: I do.

BUNSHA: You may go.

ANNA: Did you ever!

BUNSHA: Let's waste no time. You may go.

ANNA *exits.*

So much for the first try.

AVRORA (*enters*): Father! Oh, it's you! Is father out?

BUNSHA: He's out. Sit down, please, Mademoiselle Radamanov. The moment I saw you, I fell in love with you at first sight. I have reason to believe that I please you too. (*Kisses* AVRORA *on the cheek.*)

AVRORA (*slaps him*): Idiot! (*Exits.*)

BUNSHA: You're much too uppity, Avrora Pavlovna! But never mind! We'll give you a good rap on the knuckles! We know how to deal with members of society who get too high and mighty.

Enter SAVVICH.

Just the man I want.

SAVVICH: Is Pavel Sergeyevich out?

BUNSHA: He's out. May I have two words with you?

SAVVICH: Yes?

BUNSHA: I fell in love with you at first sight.

SAVVICH: What does that mean?

BUNSHA: Here's what it means. (*Takes out a slip of paper from his pocket and reads with a conspiratorial air.*) To the Director of the Institute of Harmony. On May 1st of this year, at half past twelve in the morning, Avrora Radamanova was kissing the physicist Rein. On May 3rd she and the same physicist were kissing again near this column. This very morning, at eight o'clock, said Avrora was kissing said physicist near the apparatus, at which time she spoke the following words: We shall fly away together . . .

SAVVICH: That's enough! I don't need your reports! (*Snatches the paper from* BUNSHA, *tears it up, and walks out quickly.*)

BUNSHA: That will teach Avrora Pavlovna how to slap secretaries of house committees on the cheeks!

MILOSLAVSKY (*offstage*): Is that blockhead here?

BUNSHA: He is looking for me.

MILOSLAVSKY (*enters*): Aha, there you are. I'm bored, Svyatoslav. How would you like a present of a watch? But on one condition: it must be strictly secret. Never take it out in front of anyone, and never show it to anyone.

BUNSHA: How will I be able to tell the time, then?

MILOSLAVSKY: It's not for that. Simply as a remembrance, a souvenir. What kind do you prefer, with a lid or without?

BUNSHA: Such a multitude of watches leads me to dire reflections.

MILOSLAVSKY: Just try and share your reflections with anyone! Which is it, then, with a lid?

BUNSHA: With a lid.

MILOSLAVSKY: Here you are.

BUNSHA: Thank you very much. But if you'll pardon me, this has the letter "H" on it, and my initials are "S.V.B."

MILOSLAVSKY: No complaints, please. I don't run a store. Put it away.

REIN (*enters*): Why are you here? Weren't you taken to see India?

MILOSLAVSKY: There's nothing interesting in India.

REIN: But you couldn't have been there more than five minutes.

MILOSLAVSKY: We weren't there even one minute.

REIN: Then how the devil can you say it isn't interesting?

MILOSLAVSKY: They told us all about it in the plane.

BUNSHA: Deadly monotony.

REIN: Svyatoslav Vladimirovich, you of all people ought to keep quiet! How much variety did you enjoy in your house committee? Oh, well, I have no time. (*Walks to his mechanism.*) Look here, are you planning to hang over me? I can't work like that. Go somewhere else if you don't like India.

MILOSLAVSKY: Academician! Zhenya! What's wrong with your machine? Have a heart, bring us back to where you took us from.

REIN: I am not a chauffeur.

MILOSLAVSKY: Eeh!

REIN: You are victims of chance. There's been an accident. It isn't my fault that you happened to be in Mikhelson's room. But, then, why complain? Millions of people dream of being transported to such a life. Don't you like it here?

MILOSLAVSKY: A million people may like it, and I don't. There's no scope, no application for my talents here!

REIN: What are you talking about? Why don't you recite your poems? People follow you, they look you in the mouth! And all you give them is that damned Kochubey over and over again.

MILOSLAVSKY: Eh! (*Drinks some alcohol from the faucet and smashes the glass.*)

REIN: What kind of boorishness is that?

MILOSLAVSKY: My dearest Academician! Put your brains to work! Fix your gadget and get us out of here! The streetcars are running in Moscow! People in the streets! Such fun! There's a matinee at the Bolshoi now. A crowd around the bar! Intermission time! I should be there! I pine for it! (*Drops on his knees.*)

BUNSHA (*also gets down on his knees*): Yevgeny Nikolayevich! The militia is looking all over for me. I left without permission. I'm an emigré! Take me back!

REIN: To the devil with you! Stop this circus! Can't you understand we're in trouble? The key slipped out of the machine! The key is coded. And I can't start the machine without it.

MILOSLAVSKY: What? Did you say, the key? You mean the little gold key?

REIN: Exactly, the little gold key.

MILOSLAVSKY: And you kept quiet for two weeks! (*Embraces* REIN.) Hurrah! Hurrah! Hurrah!

REIN: Leave me alone, will you! It has twenty digits on it, and I can't remember them!

MILOSLAVSKY: Why do you need to remember them when the key is in your pocket?

REIN: It isn't there. (*Feels in his pockets, brings out the key.*) What is this? I don't understand anything. It's magic!

BUNSHA: The chain of my suspicions is about to close.

REIN: Avrora! Avrora!

AVRORA (*enters*): What? What is it?

REIN (*showing her*): The key!

AVRORA: My legs are trembling . . . Where was it?

REIN: I can't understand it . . . In my pocket . . .

AVRORA: In your pocket! In your pocket!

MILOSLAVSKY: Let's fly at once!

REIN: Sorry, I need twenty-four hours to regulate the mechanism. And if you keep jumping in front of my eyes, it will take longer. Please go, the two of you.

MILOSLAVSKY: We're going, we're going. But, please, work, don't be distracted by anything.

REIN: I'll beg you not to give me any instructions.

AVRORA (*to* MILOSLAVSKY): And not a word to anyone that the key has been found.

MILOSLAVSKY: You can be sure of that, not a sound . . . (*To* BUNSHA.) Follow me, and keep your mouth shut! (*Exits with* BUNSHA.)

REIN: The key! Avrora, the key! (*Embraces her.*)

MILOSLAVSKY (*peeking in*): I beg you, Zhenechka, no distractions . . . Pardon, mademoiselle. I'm gone, I'm gone, I'm gone . . . I just looked in for a moment, and now I'm gone.

Darkness. The same terrace. REIN *and* AVRORA *at the machine.* REIN *is regulating it, and the ring begins to glimmer from time to time.*

REIN: Do you hear?

AVRORA: It hums.

The signal flashes in the communication apparatus.
REIN *extinguishes the ring of light and puts the key in his pocket.*

Hush . . . It's father. (*Exits.*)

RADAMANOV (*enters*): Good morning, Rein. Forgive me for disturbing you at work, but I have something of extreme importance to tell you.

REIN: I am at your service.

RADAMANOV: I just come from a meeting that was devoted to you.

REIN: Yes?

RADAMANOV: And I was asked to convey this message to you. We have resolved that your invention is of the utmost state importance. And you, as the author of the invention, are to be placed in entirely exceptional conditions and given every privilege. All your needs and all your wishes will be satisfied in full, whatever they may be. I have nothing to add to this except to congratulate you.

REIN: I beg you to convey my deepest gratitude to the Council of People's Commissars. I am also thankful for the hospitality shown to me and to my chance companions.

RADAMANOV: I shall be glad to transmit all this. And this is all you wish to say?

REIN: Yes, it is . . . I am most flattered . . .

RADAMANOV: I must confess to you, I expected more. If I were in your place, I would have said that I am grateful to the state and that I beg it to accept my invention as a gift.

REIN: You mean . . . You want me to give you my machine?

RADAMANOV: I beg you to think about it. Could it be otherwise?

REIN: Ah! I am beginning to understand. Tell me, if I repair my machine . . .

RADAMANOV: Of which I have no doubt.

REIN: Will I be given an opportunity to fly it by myself?

RADAMANOV: With us, with us, my brilliant friend!

REIN: The People's Commissar of Inventions! I see it all now! Well, if you please, here is my machine, you can have it. But I warn you, I will lie down on the sofa and will not take a step in its direction while there is even a single person here to watch me.

RADAMANOV: I don't believe you, I don't believe you. If you do this, you will die in the shortest possible time.

REIN: Do you intend to stop feeding me?

RADAMANOV: Truly, you are a child of another century. Stop feeding a man like you? Eat all you wish. But a moment will come when you will not be able to get a bite of food into your mouth, and you will waste away. A man who has accomplished what you have accomplished cannot lie down on the sofa.

REIN: This machine belongs to me.

RADAMANOV: What musty, though interesting, antiquity speaks with your lips! It would belong to you, Rein, if you were the only man on earth. But now it belongs to all.

REIN: If you'll allow me! I am a man of another era. I beg you to let me go, I am your guest by chance.

RADAMANOV: My dear, I would call anyone who did so a madman! No era would let you go, and none will, believe me!

REIN: I don't see why you need this machine.

RADAMANOV: You don't? I can't believe it. You don't strike me as a feeble-minded man. The very first turn of the key, and that . . . what's his name . . . Vasily the Terrible . . . is rushing around in your Moscow out there . . . Did he live in the nineteenth century?

REIN: He lived in the sixteenth, and his name is Ivan.

RADAMANOV: I beg your pardon, I don't know history too well. That's Avrora's field. Well, then. You've left everything in turmoil behind you. And then you may blunder into the twenty-sixth century . . . And who, besides Savvich, who is certain that the twenty-sixth century will inevitably be better than our twenty-third, will vouch for what you'll find there? Who knows whom you might bring back to us from that mysterious distance on your own? But that isn't all. Can you imagine what benefits we may reap if *we* make our way into other periods? Your machine can do four hundred years, you say?

REIN: Yes, approximately.

RADAMANOV: That means it can reach infinity. And then, who knows! Even in our own lifetime we may see the freezing earth and the dying sun above it! This invention belongs to all! They all live now, and I serve them! Oh, Rein!

REIN: I see. I am a prisoner. You will not let me go. But I am curious to know how you propose to control me. After all, you will not assign a militiaman to guard me?

RADAMANOV: The only militiaman you can find here is under glass in the museum in the Azure Vertical, and he has been there for more than a hundred years. Incidentally, I've heard that your friend Miloslavsky, after a good many drinks, visited the museum yesterday and wept tender tears over the exhibit. Oh, well, every man to his taste . . . No, my dear, you are too intelligent to be taught the abc's! We ask you to give us your invention of your own good will. Give up your century, become a citizen of ours. And the state invites you to join us in all the flights we shall make. Your hand, Rein!

REIN: I surrender the machine, you have convinced me.

RADAMANOV (*shakes* REIN's *hand and opens the glass case*):
I shall keep one key to the case; the other will be given
to Savvich, who has been appointed the second in control. Tomorrow I shall send to you specialists in the
restoration of memory. Before three days are out you
will find your code, I promise you.

REIN: Wait before you lock it, Radamanov. I don't need
any specialists. The key with the code has been found,
here it is. I can start the mechanism tomorrow.

RADAMANOV: I respect you, Rein. Your hand. (*Takes the
key.*)

AVRORA (*runs in*): Give me the key, this very minute! What
did you do! I knew you needed a nursemaid!

RADAMANOV: Have you gone mad? You were eavesdropping!

AVRORA: I heard everything, to the last word. To say goodbye to my dreams of seeing everything we planned to
see! . . . I want you to know, father, that Rein will
not fly without me! Isn't that true, Rein?

REIN: It's true.

AVRORA: He is my husband, father! Remember that! We
love each other!

RADAMANOV (*to* REIN): You have become her husband? In
your place I would have thought it over very carefully
before taking the step. But then, it's your private affair. (*To* AVRORA.) I'll beg you to stop shouting.

REIN: Pavel Sergeyevich . . .

AVRORA: I will not stop!

REIN: Pavel Sergeyevich, you told me that my wishes would
be fulfilled?

RADAMANOV: Yes, I said it. And since I said it once, I can
repeat it.

REIN: Well then, I want Avrora to fly with me.

AVRORA: Now you speak like a man!

RADAMANOV: She will fly with you.

AVRORA (*to* REIN): Demand that your first flight be into your old life! I want to see your room! And Ivan the Terrible!

RADAMANOV: She will fly with you. But before you fly with her, I would suggest you inquire into her character.

AVRORA: Shut up, right now.

RADAMANOV: No, you shut up, I have not finished yet. (*Takes a small box from his pocket.*) We beg you to accept this gift—a chronometer. It is inscribed: To the engineer Rein, from the World Council of People's Commissars. (*Opens the box.*) But wait! Where is it? The only man I showed it to was Miloslavsky, and he clapped his hands with admiration! No, this is altogether too much!

The signal flashes on the table, the trap opens, and SAVVICH *appears.*

SAVVICH: I am here, as agreed.

RADAMANOV: Yes. Here is the machine. And this is the key. It's been found. Please lock the case.

SAVVICH: So the machine can be started?

RADAMANOV: Yes, it can.

They lock the case.

AVRORA (*to* SAVVICH): Ferdinand, Rein is my husband, and I want you to know that I will fly with him.

SAVVICH: No, Avrora. That will not be so soon. Listen to the decision of the Institute of Harmony. On the basis of studies of the brains of these three individuals, who have come to us from the twentieth century, the Institute has resolved that they must be isolated for treatment for the period of a year, because, Radamanov, they are a menace to our society. And I wish you to know that all the recent losses have been explained. The objects have been stolen by this company. These people are defective. Avrora and Rein, we are separating you.

AVRORA: Oh, so that's how it is! Father, take an admiring look at the director of the Institute of Harmony! Look at him! He is in a rage because he lost me!

SAVVICH: Avrora, don't insult me. I have done my duty. He cannot live in Bliss!

REIN (*to* SAVVICH): What did you say about the lost articles? (*Seizes a paperweight from the table.*)

RADAMANOV: Rein! Put down the paperweight! I order you! (*To* SAVVICH.) I'm sick of your Institute of Harmony! And I shall prove to you most convincingly that I am sick of it.

REIN: Radamanov! I am sorry I gave you the key!

SAVVICH: Goodbye. (*Descends into the trap.*)

RADAMANOV: Rein, wait for me, and calm yourself. I am taking this upon myself. (*Exits.*)

AVRORA (*runs after him*): Father! Tell them that . . . (*Disappears.*)

REIN (*alone*): So that's how it is . . . that's how it is . . .

Enter MILOSLAVSKY *and* BUNSHA.

MILOSLAVSKY: Well, Professor, is the machine ready?

REIN: I want the chronometer, this minute!

MILOSLAVSKY: The chronometer? The one with the inscription? Why, here it is, on the table. Right here . . .

BUNSHA: Now my suspicions have turned into certainty.

REIN: Get out, both of you! And if you meet Savvich, tell him to stay out of my way!

Darkness.

ACT FOUR

The same day. The same terrace.

ANNA: Dear Zhorzh, I am so upset! Can I do anything to ease your suffering?

MILOSLAVSKY: You can. Hit your disgusting Savvich on the head with a brick.

ANNA: Your images are so graphic, Zhorzh.

MILOSLAVSKY: These aren't images. And you haven't heard the really graphic ones yet. Eh, if I could let loose with a string of proper oaths now, maybe I'd feel better.

ANNA: Let loose then, Zhorzh!

MILOSLAVSKY: You think so? What the devil! . . . No . . . It's somehow awkward here. Such decent surroundings . . .

ANNA: Zhorzh, I don't believe you are a criminal.

MILOSLAVSKY: Who will believe it?

ANNA: Oh, I like you so much, Zhorzh!

MILOSLAVSKY: All the women like me.

ANNA: You're so cruel.

MILOSLAVSKY: Annette, why don't you better go and try to hear what they're saying at their meeting.

ANNA: What are you asking me to do!

MILOSLAVSKY: Well, as you wish . . . I may be lost, but first, in dazzling hope, I must . . .

ANNA: Is this your own poem?

MILOSLAVSKY: My own.

ANNA: I go. (*Exits.*)

147

BUNSHA *enters.*

MILOSLAVSKY: Did you hear anything?
BUNSHA: No, I climbed up on the column, but they noticed me.
MILOSLAVSKY: What an ass!
BUNSHA: I'm in despair myself.

Pause.

GRABBE: May I come in?
MILOSLAVSKY: A-ah, Doctor! Certainly. What's the good word, Doctor?
GRABBE: Unfortunately, there is little good to report. The Institute has instructed me, first, to inform you of the results of your examinations, and, second, to place you in treatment. (*Hands an envelope each to* MILOSLAVSKY *and* BUNSHA.)
MILOSLAVSKY: Merci. (*Reads.*) Please lend me your pince-nez for a moment, I cannot make out a word here.
GRABBE: Certainly.
MILOSLAVSKY: Here . . . What does this mean—klepto-mania?
GRABBE: A morbid desire to steal.
MILOSLAVSKY: Ah. I thank you. Merci.
BUNSHA: May I borrow your pince-nez too? What is this—de-mentia?
GRABBE: Feeble-mindedness.

BUNSHA *returns the pince-nez.*

MILOSLAVSKY: Merci, for both of us. But who's the rat who made the diagnosis?
GRABBE: If you pardon me, it was the world-famous Professor Murphy of London.

MILOSLAVSKY (*into the apparatus*): London, please. Merci. Professor Murphy, please. Merci.

A *voice in the apparatus*: Do you need a translator?

No, we don't. Professor Murphy? You are not a professor, Murphy, you're a louse. (*Shuts off the signal.*)
GRABBE: What are you doing?
MILOSLAVSKY: Silence! Three times I've had my fingerprints taken—in Moscow, in Leningrad, and in Rostov-on-the-Don. And all the chiefs of criminal investigation said unanimously that a man with such a finger could not steal. And suddenly there's this faker, this horse-doctor . . .
GRABBE: Collect yourself! Bunsha, try to influence your friend . . .
BUNSHA: Silence!
GRABBE (*into the apparatus*): Savvich!

SAVVICH *appears*.

GRABBE: I refuse to treat them. Turn them over to another doctor. (*Leaves.*)
SAVVICH (*to* MILOSLAVSKY): You insulted Professor Grabbe? Wait, you'll be sorry!
MILOSLAVSKY: I insulted him? He insulted me! And also my best friend, Svyatoslav Vladimirovich Bunsha-Koretsky, former prince and secretary! What kind of a word is this—kleptomania? I ask you, what kind of a word is this—kleptomania?
SAVVICH: I'll beg you not to shout!
MILOSLAVSKY: I am whispering! What does it mean—kleptomania?
SAVVICH: Ah, you don't know? I'll tell you what it means. It's when gold things suddenly begin to disappear in

Bliss . . . That's what it means! Tell me, please, you haven't chanced to come across my cigarette case?

MILOSLAVSKY: A little gold one, with the letter "S" on the corner?

SAVVICH: Yes, yes, exactly!

MILOSLAVSKY: No, I haven't come across it.

SAVVICH: Where is it, then?

MILOSLAVSKY: Cigarette cases should be locked away, young man. And you leave them all over on tables, leading people into temptation. And then they have to suffer because of you! Look at this finger! Can a man with such a finger steal anything? Do you know anything about this science—dactiloscopy? Ah, you haven't read that far? All you've learned about is kleptomania. When my finger was examined at the Moscow Criminal Investigation Department people from all the other offices came running to see it! This finger cannot touch a single thing that belongs to somebody else! Here is your cigarette case, choke on it! Here! (*Throws the cigarette case to* SAVVICH.)

SAVVICH: A fine company was brought to Bliss by the engineer Rein! And just when this man is caught with somebody else's belongings, Radamanov in the kindness of his heart tries to defend him! No, it will not be! You've hurt your own cause! (*Exits.*)

BUNSHA: I thought he'd quiet down after your speech, but he got even more excited.

REIN *and* AVRORA *come hurrying in.*

Yevgeny Nikolayevich! I have been cruelly insulted.

REIN: Be quiet, please. I've no time for your nonsense. Go out for a moment, I have to talk things over with Avrora.

BUNSHA: Such insults can only be washed off with blood.

REIN: Get out, both of you!

BUNSHA *and* MILOSLAVSKY *exit.*

Speak, Avrora, we have little time.

AVRORA: We must escape!

REIN: What? Break my word to Radamanov? I made a promise!

AVRORA: Let's fly! I won't permit them to push you around! I hate Savvich!

REIN: You do? But think, Avrora, I give you only a few seconds! You'll have to leave Bliss, probably forever! You will never return here!

AVRORA: I'm sick of these columns, I'm sick of Savvich, I'm sick of Bliss! I've never experienced danger, I don't know the taste of it! Let's fly!

REIN: Where?

AVRORA: To you!

REIN: Miloslavsky!

MILOSLAVSKY *and* BUNSHA *appear.*

MILOSLAVSKY: Here I am!

REIN: I want to have the keys from the case, at once! One is in Radamanov's pocket, the other in Savvich's.

MILOSLAVSKY: Zhenya! With this finger a man cannot steal . . .

REIN: Oh, he can't! Very well, then, you can stay in that hospital!

MILOSLAVSKY: . . . cannot steal at the meeting, because they won't let him in. But he can open any cabinet.

REIN: Idiot! This cabinet has a triple-coded lock!

MILOSLAVSKY: Such cabinets are never locked with kitchen

locks. You're an idiot yourself, Zhenechka. Bunsha, on the lookout! If you let anybody in I'll kill you. (*To* REIN.) A penknife, if you please. (*Takes the knife from* REIN *and opens the first lock.*)

AVRORA (*to* REIN): Did you see?

MILOSLAVSKY: Bunsha, sleeping on duty? I'll knock your head off! (*Throws the cabinet wide open.*)

ANNA (*runs in*): They have resolved . . . What are you doing?

MILOSLAVSKY: It makes no difference now what they have resolved!

ANNA: You're a madman! This is a confidential government case! So they spoke the truth! You are a criminal!

MILOSLAVSKY: Anuta, shh!

REIN *takes his machine from the cabinet and regulates it.*

ANNA: Avrora, stop them! Make them see the light!

AVRORA: I'm flying with them.

MILOSLAVSKY: Anyutochka, come with me!

ANNA: No, no! I'm afraid! It's a terrible crime!

MILOSLAVSKY: Well, as you wish. Be brave at the trial! Blame everything on me alone! And whatever the judge will ask you, say one thing: I was drunk, I don't remember anything! They will reduce your sentence!

ANNA: I cannot bear to see this! (*Runs out.*)

MILOSLAVSKY (*after her*): If it's a boy, call him Zhorzh! In my honor! Bunsha! Pack up!

REIN: Don't dare to take anything from the cabinet!

MILOSLAVSKY: Oh, no! There's a little flying gadget here that I must take along!

Alarm signals are sounded. Voices are heard in the

distance. And a steel wall drops down, cutting off the way from the platform.

REIN: What's this?
AVRORA: Hurry! It's the alarm! The cabinet gave an alarm signal! Hurry!

The ring flares up around the time machine. A burst of music.

MILOSLAVSKY: The Bolshoi Theater! I'll just make it for the last act!
BUNSHA (*seizes Mikhelson's clock and rushes toward the machine*): I am an official, I go first!
MILOSLAVSKY: The devil with you!
REIN: One at a time. (*Switches on the mechanism.*)

A wind sweeps across the room, the light dims for a moment, and BUNSHA *disappears.*

MILOSLAVSKY: Anyuta! Think of me! (*Disappears.*)

The trap opens and SAVVICH *emerges.*

SAVVICH: Ah, I see! The siren! The siren! They broke the cabinet open! They're escaping! Radamanov! (*Rushes toward them, trying to hold them back. Catches* AVRORA *by the hand.*)
REIN (*snatches an automatic revolver from the cabinet, fires into the air.*)

SAVVICH *lets go of* AVRORA's *hand.*

REIN: Savvich! I warned you to stay out of my way! One move and I'll shoot you!

SAVVICH: This is base force! I am unarmed! Avrora!

AVRORA: I detest you!

Another trap opens, and RADAMANOV *appears.*

SAVVICH: Radamanov! Look out! There's a murderer here!
He'll shoot you!

RADAMANOV: I am not afraid.

SAVVICH: I cannot detain him. He is armed!

RADAMANOV: Then he should not be detained. (*To* REIN,
pointing at the cabinet.) How is that, engineer Rein?

REIN (*pointing at* SAVVICH): He is the one to blame. (*Takes
out the chronometer.*) I have the chronometer. Miloslavsky gave it to me! I return it to you, Pavel Sergeyevich! I have no right to it. Farewell! We shall never
meet again!

RADAMANOV: Who knows, who knows, engineer Rein!

REIN: Farewell!

AVRORA: Father! Farewell!

RADAMANOV: Goodbye! Till we meet again, Mr. and Mrs.
Rein! When you get tired of flying, come back to us!

RADAMANOV *presses a button and the steel wall rises,
opening the view upon the colonnade and the sky of
Bliss.* REIN *throws away the revolver, switches on the
mechanism. A burst of music. He snatches up the machine. The light dims.* REIN *and* AVRORA *disappear.*

SAVVICH: Radamanov! What shall I do! They're gone!

RADAMANOV: It's your fault! And you shall answer for it,
Savvich!

SAVVICH: Avrora! Come back!

Darkness.

REIN'S *room. The same day and hour as when our heroes took off for Bliss. On the stage are* MIKHELSON, *very upset, and the militia. The* MILITIA OFFICER *is writing a report.*

OFFICER: Whom do you suspect, citizen?

MIKHELSON: Everybody. All the tenants in the house are crooks, swindlers, and counter-revolutionaries.

OFFICER: Quite a house!

MIKHELSON: Arrest them all! Right down the line, the whole list! And the small building in the yard is also full of criminals from top to bottom.

OFFICER: Without panic, citizen. (*Examines the tenants' list.*) Let's see who lives here, now. Bunsha-Koretsky?

MIKHELSON: A thief!

OFFICER: Engineer Rein?

MIKHELSON: A thief!

OFFICER: This woman, citizen Podrezkova?

MIKHELSON: A thief!

OFFICER: Citizen Mikhelson?

MIKHELSON: That's me, the victim. Arrest everybody except me.

OFFICER: No panic, please.

A sudden blast of wind, the light goes out and flares up. BUNSHA *appears, with* MIKHELSON'S *clock in his hands.*

MIKHELSON: There he is! Grab him, comrades! My clock!

BUNSHA: Comrades! Secretary Bunsha-Koretsky, returned of his own free will, to resume his duties! I beg you to make a special note of it in the report: of his own free will. I rescued your clock, most esteemed citizen Mikhelson.

OFFICER (*to* BUNSHA): Where did you come from? You are under arrest, citizen.

BUNSHA: I turn myself over with pleasure into the hands of my native militia, and I make an important announcement: in the attic . . .

The light goes out. Thunder and music, and MILO-SLAVSKY *appears.*

MIKHELSON: Comrades, my coat!

MILOSLAVSKY (*jumps up on the window, throws it open, pulls off* MIKHELSON's *coat*): Here's your coat, citizen Mikhelson! You can take it to the store where they sell old rags! I borrowed it temporarily! And here's your pocket watch and your cigarette case! You haven't the slightest idea of what kind of coats and cigarette cases exist in the world! As for stealing, I'm incapable of it! Look at this finger! Bunsha, goodbye! Write me in Rostov!

MIKHELSON: Hold him!

BUNSHA: Zhorshik! Give yourself up to the militia with me and repent sincerely!

MILOSLAVSKY: Grand merci. Au revoir! (*Unfolds the flying apparatus he brought from Bliss and flies away.*)

BUNSHA: Gone! Flew away! Comrades! In the attic . . .

OFFICER: You'll have your say later!

Music. The light goes out. REIN *and* AVRORA *appear.*

MIKHELSON: More members of the gang!

REIN: Citizen Mikhelson! You're a blockhead! Avrora, calm down, don't be afraid of anything!

AVRORA: Who are these men in cloth helmets?

REIN: The militia. (*To the militiamen.*) I am the engineer

Rein. I invented a time machine and have just been in the future. This woman is my wife. I beg you to be gentle with her, don't frighten her.

MIKHELSON: I've been robbed, and they're not to be frightened!

OFFICER: Your case will have to wait a moment, citizen! Is this the apparatus that the tsar came out of?

BUNSHA: That's it, that's it! It was I who called you! He's holed up in the attic now, I've been trying to tell you!

OFFICER: Comrade Mostovoy! Comrade Zhudilov!

Movement on the stage. The door leading to the attic opens and everybody recoils. IVAN THE TERRIBLE *walks in, in a state of quiet derangement. Seeing the group, he crosses himself.*

IVAN: O, grievous fortune! . . . Lord God and Saintly Fathers, I pray to you, half-monk that I am . . .

Pause.

MIKHELSON: Comrades! Grab him! Who does he think he is!

IVAN (*turns a dim eye on* MIKHELSON): Dog! Mortal pimple!

MIKHELSON: Oh, so I'm a pimple too!

AVRORA (*to* REIN): God, how interesting! What will they do with him? Send him back. He's gone mad!

REIN: Yes. I will.

Switches on the machine. The tolling of the tocsin. IVAN's *vaulted chamber comes into view. The* CAPTAIN OF THE MUSKETEERS *rushes about desperately.*

CAPTAIN: Hey, musketeers! Hundreder! Hey-ho! Where's the Tsar?

REIN (*to* IVAN): Into your chamber!

IVAN: Lord! Lord! (*Rushes into the chamber.*)

REIN *switches off the mechanism. The royal chamber vanishes, and with it* IVAN *and the* CAPTAIN OF THE MUSKETEERS.

OFFICER (*to* REIN): You are under arrest, citizen. Follow us.

REIN: With pleasure. Avrora, don't be afraid.

BUNSHA: Don't be afraid, Avrora Pavlovna, our militia are kind.

MIKHELSON: But, comrades, what about my robbery?

OFFICER: Your robbery is postponed, for the time being, citizen. This is a bit more important than a robbery!

The MILITIAMEN *lead away* REIN, AVRORA, *and* BUNSHA.

MIKHELSON (*alone, after a stupefied silence*): My watch, my cigarette case, here . . . my coat . . . Everything's here . . . (*Pause.*) Well, comrades, such are the things that came to pass in our Bathhouse Lane. And yet, if I should tell the story to the fellows at the office, they won't believe me, no, not for the life of me, they won't!

Darkness

MIRRA GINSBURG was born in Russia and came to the United States as a child. She has translated and edited works by a good friend of Bulgakov's, Yevgeny Zamyatin (*We*, a novel, *The Dragon: Fifteen Stories*, and *A Soviet Heretic*, a collection of essays), as well as novels and stories by Fyodor Dostoyevsky, Alexey Remizov, Isaac Babel, Isaac Bashevis Singer, Zoshchenko, Ilf and Petrov, Andrey Platonov, and others. Among the works of Bulgakov, she has translated *The Master and Margarita*, *The Fatal Eggs*, *Heart of a Dog*, and *The Life of Monsieur de Molière*. She is also the translator and editor of many collections of folklore, and the author of more than twenty books for children.